Institute of Leadership
& Management

superseries

Achieving
Objectives
Through Time
Management

FIFTH EDITION

Published for the
Institute of Leadership & Management

AMSTERDAM • BOSTON • HEIDELBERG • LONDON • NEW YORK • OXFORD
PARIS • SAN DIEGO • SAN FRANCISCO • SINGAPORE • SYDNEY • TOKYO
Pergamon Flexible Learning is an imprint of Elsevier

ELSEVIER

Pergamon
Flexible
Learning

Pergamon Flexible Learning is an imprint of Elsevier
Linacre House, Jordan Hill, Oxford OX2 8DP, UK
30 Corporate Drive, Suite 400, Burlington, MA 01803, USA

First edition 1986
Second edition 1991
Third edition 1997
Fourth edition 2003
Fifth edition 2007

British Library Cataloguing in Publication Data
A catalogue record for this book is available from the British Library

Library of Congress Cataloguing in Publication Data
A catalogue record for this book is available from the Library of Congress

ISBN 978-0-08-046415-2

For information on all Pergamon Flexible Learning publications
visit our website at http://books.elsevier.com

Institute of Leadership & Management
Registered Office
1 Giltspur Street
London
EC1A 9DD
Telephone: 020 7294 2470
www.i-l-m.com
ILM is part of the City & Guilds Group

Typeset by Charon Tec Ltd (A Macmillan Company), Chennai, India
www.charontec.com
Printed and bound in Great Britain

07 08 09 10 11   10 9 8 7 6 5 4 3 2 1

Contents

Series preface

Whether you are a tutor/trainer or studying management development to further your career, Super Series provides an exciting and flexible resource to help you to achieve your goals. The fifth edition is completely new and up-to-date, and has been structured to perfectly match the Institute of Leadership & Management (ILM)'s new unit-based qualifications for first line managers. It also harmonizes with the 2004 national occupational standards in management and leadership, providing an invaluable resource for S/NVQs at Level 3 in Management.

Super Series is equally valuable for anyone tutoring or studying any management programmes at this level, whether leading to a qualification or not. Individual workbooks also support short programmes, which may be recognized by ILM as Endorsed or Development Awards, or provide the ideal way to undertake CPD activities.

For learners, coping with all the pressures of today's world, Super Series offers you the flexibility to study at your own pace to fit around your professional and other commitments. You don't need a PC or to attend classes at a specific time – choose when and where to study to suit yourself! And you will always have the complete workbook as a quick reference just when you need it.

For tutors/trainers, Super Series provides an invaluable guide to what needs to be covered, and in what depth. It also allows learners who miss occasional sessions to 'catch up' by dipping into the series.

Super Series provides unrivalled support for all those involved in first line management and supervision.

Unit specification

Title:	Achieving objectives through time management		Unit Ref:	M3.04
Level:	3			
Credit value:	1			

Learning outcomes *The learner will*	Assessment criteria *The learner can (in an organization with which the learner is familiar)*	
1. Understand the importance of effective time management in prioritizing and achieving objectives	1.1	Set SMART objectives for own workload, list them in order of priority and establish appropriate time scales for their achievement
	1.2	Plan the achievement of the objectives using an established time management technique
	1.3	Identify constraining or limiting factors that could hinder the achievement of any one of these objectives
	1.4	Briefly explain the monitoring techniques for any objective

Workbook introduction

1 ILM Super Series 4 study links

This workbook addresses the issues of *Achieving Objectives Through Time Management*. Should you wish to extend your study to other Super Series workbooks covering related or different subject areas, you will find a comprehensive list at the back of this book.

2 Links to ILM qualifications

This workbook relates to the learning outcomes of Unit M3.04 Achieving objectives through time management from the ILM Level 3 Award, Certificate and Diploma in First Line Management.

3 Links to S/NVQs in management

This workbook relates to the following Unit of the Management Standards used in S/NVQs in Management, as well as a range of other S/NVQs:

A2   Managing self and other skills

4 Workbook objectives

Do you believe you could achieve more if only you had the time? Does most of your time get used up by the demands of others? Do you wish you were more in control of your time?

Of all resources available to the manager, time is the most precious and the hardest to use well. When we lose time it can never be replaced. When we abuse it, we are the ones to suffer. If ever we gain some time, we may not find any use for it, except to kill it.

As this workbook suggests, to save time you have to spend time: you must take time in order to learn how to use time to your advantage.

The one thing you can be sure of is that if you don't manage and control your own time, you will find it much harder to control and manage everything else.

We begin by investigating some typical 'activity traps' – habits of behaviour at work in which time gets used up without the user having much say about it. To escape from these traps, it's important to take control over your own time.

In the next session, we examine the process of making decisions, and the importance of getting the timing right. Then we'll consider the typical demands made on the manager's time; who makes these demands, and what the response should be. Then we return to the subject of habits: getting into good ones and avoiding bad ones. The last part of the session is devoted to the management grid, a device that is useful in determining how urgent and how important a particular task is.

The third session of the workbook is called 'Making time work'. It discusses some useful time management techniques. The final session goes on to propose some ways of dealing with unexpected events. We conclude with a discussion about time management problems and about ways to get time management accepted by other people.

4.1 Objectives

At the end of this workbook you should be better able to:

1   identify ways of increasing efficiency and effectiveness by setting objectives and through better time management;

2   differentiate between the demands on the time available, and agree and set priorities;

3   realize more of your and your team's goals by utilizing available time more effectively;

4   Employ appropriate time management techniques that can support the use of your own and your team's time.

Session A
Where does all the time go?

1 Introduction

How often have you said: 'I wish there were more time in the day'?

There are always deadlines to meet, problems to deal with, demands upon your time.

But, if we're honest, many of us would have to admit that we don't stop to think about making better use of our time. We get into certain patterns of working, we find a way of coping from day to day, and are content to let things go on as they are.

In this first session of the workbook, we will look in more depth at some of the unthinking behaviour that leads to these unrewarding work patterns.

First, though, we'll try to define our subject.

2 What is time management?

Let us begin by defining what we mean by 'managing time' or 'time management'.

Activity 1

3 mins

What do you understand by 'managing time'? Spend a few minutes thinking about it and then write down your own definition – in no more than a sentence or two, if you can.

_____

_____

_____

_____

Some examples of how 'managing time' have been described are:

■ making the best use of time;
■ getting more done in the time available;
■ not wasting time on irrelevant things;
■ getting more control over time;
■ spending more time on the important parts of the job;
■ avoiding a last-minute rush to get things done.

These are all correct. You may have defined 'managing time' in a different way.

In general, managing something implies having **control** over it and making **decisions** about it. So, one good definition would be:

Managing time means taking more control over how you spend your time and making sensible decisions about the way you use it.

When thinking about how to manage your time, it is useful to distinguish between things you want to achieve in the short term and those you want to achieve in the longer term. So we usually make a distinction between short-term **objectives** and longer-term **goals.**

Objectives tend to be concrete and immediate, and can be formulated as a series of tasks (we will look at how to draw up objectives later in this session).

Goals, on the other hand, may be made up of a number of different objectives. For example, the sales and the production departments of a large company have different objectives, but they both work towards achieving the organization's overall and longer-term goals, which are the same for all departments.

It is also worth distinguishing between objectives and goals **at work** and your own **personal** goals and objectives. The two may sometimes overlap. For example, taking on a more challenging task at work may help to achieve the department's objectives, but it may also contribute to fulfilling a longer-term goal of your own, by providing you with a valuable opportunity to learn a new (and transferable) skill.

3 Activity traps

Many managers and team leaders find themselves in patterns of working that seem to prevent any means of escape: each day is filled with activities which, for one reason or another, don't seem to lead anywhere. This results in a feeling of not being able to control one's time – or one's working life. A good name for these ineffective and frustrating working patterns is **activity traps**.

EXTENSIONS 1–5
The books listed here all contain many useful suggestions related to better management of time.

We're going to look now at three kinds of activity trap. As you read through the following three sections, ask yourself whether, and to what extent, the situation described applies to you.

Also, bear in mind the following important questions. These are the keys to escaping from each trap.

What are you trying to achieve?

What stands in the way of your achieving it?

4 Activity trap 1: crisis management

Kris works in a company that makes and sells electrical meters. He describes his job as 'fire-fighting'. No sooner is one crisis over than another one flares up.

'I never seem to have a spare minute from the time I arrive till the time I go home. Management always want everything to be done yesterday. It's: "There's a problem here, Kris. Sort it out, will you?" Or: "Can you just check on stocks here, Kris, it's vital!" Or: "We need to get these orders to customers by Wednesday, Kris. It's urgent — top priority!" I tell you — everything is always top priority here.'

This kind of rushing from one crisis to the next, coping with whatever problem is most pressing at the time, is often called 'fire-fighting'.

Activity 2

3 mins

What are likely to be the effects of this pattern of working on Kris? Try to think of **two** consequences.

_____

_____

_____

_____

Some effects of this approach to work are as follows.

■ It causes **stress**.

Because he is always dealing with things in a rush, Kris is likely to suffer from stress. Although a certain amount of stress does no harm, too much stress can raise the blood pressure and make us more prone to illness.

■ It tends to result in **mistakes** and errors of judgement.

When everything is done in a panic, decisions must be taken with insufficient time for thought. There's no time to prepare and there's no time to check on results.

■ It causes **fatigue** and saps energy.

In an emergency situation, the adrenaline flows — we find extra energy to deal with the crisis. But when the panic's over, our bodies need more rest. Dealing with one crisis after another can be very wearing indeed, which is another reason why mistakes occur.

Another description of Kris's activities would be 'crisis management'.

A crisis is: 'a crucial state of affairs, requiring urgent action, whose outcome will have a decisive effect for better or worse'.

Crisis management is a trap because time is used up dealing with urgent problems that can't be postponed. People get out of the habit of planning their work, and so have no alternative but to lurch from one crisis to the next.

Of course, crises occur from time to time in the best of companies. Well-run organizations, however, try to avoid crises. Apart from the effects on individuals, which we listed above, crises are often **very** expensive.

As an example: if Kris's store is dealing with a shipment that 'must reach the customers by Wednesday' they may have to pay people to work overtime, and are likely to use the quickest – and therefore most costly – method of transport.

Some people seem to enjoy crises.

Activity 3 · 3 mins

What's the attraction of crisis management as a way of operating? Jot down **two** reasons why people often enjoy dealing with crises.

_____

_____

_____

_____

The reasons include:

- the excitement;
- the feeling of importance that people get: a crisis attracts attention;
- the sense of achievement, once the crisis is over;
- the fact that it is often easier to get people to do things, and resources allotted, when the situation is seen to be critical.

Another reason that some managers fall into the crisis management activity trap is that it is very easy to do so.

To become a crisis manager, simply do nothing.

A crisis will occur sooner or later.

This gives us a clue about the way to avoid crises.

Activity 4

3 mins

What approach could Kris take, in order to get out of the crisis management activity trap? Briefly write down any advice you could give to help him try to get out of this pattern of working.

_____

_____

_____

_____

'There cannot be a crisis next week. My schedule is already full.' – Henry Kissinger, in the *New York Times*; 1 June 1969.

We have to assume, first of all, that the situation Kris finds himself in is not all of his own making. So, like most of us, he has only limited control over his own circumstances.

Nevertheless, there's quite a lot he might do, such as:

■ point out to his manager the fact that crises cost money;
■ request that he be given the maximum possible notice of work to be done – perhaps a schedule, so that he can plan to deal with things in a sensible order;
■ agree a list of priorities with his manager;
■ question whether every crisis is real: when an organization is constantly dealing with urgent cases, the people trying to get routine tasks done may feel they have to compete by stressing urgency where none exists.

Activity 5

3 mins

What happens in your workplace once a crisis is over? Does everyone breathe a sigh of relief and forget about it, or do you start thinking how you can avoid the same crisis happening again?

_____

_____

_____

_____

You might think about the way you can benefit from a crisis once it is over. Perhaps you might hold a meeting or investigation to analyse why the crisis occurred?

If you **do** enjoy crises, have you thought about the consequences of crises on the team and on the organization?

5 Activity trap 2: responding to demands

Aysen is a team leader in a busy supermarket, in charge of a workteam of 14 shop assistants. Aysen is responsible to the store manager, Margaret. She is also supposed to liaise with the deputy store manager, Kolfi, on staffing details, stocks and customer information.

When the supermarket is busy, such as on a Saturday morning, all of Aysen's workteam are on the check-out tills or at the counters. Aysen spends most of her time near the tills dealing with any problems. At quieter times of the week there may be only two people on the tills and Aysen may supervise the re-stocking of shelves or hold meetings with Margaret or Kolfi. She finds that her shift always passes quickly. On most days she walks many miles around the store from one section to the next, dealing with minor problems, requests, queries, checking in at the office and at the store-room. As she says: 'Towards the end of the week, there's not much time to sit down and think about what I'm doing. I have to be available for all my team members, and then there are the reps and, of course, the customers. I'm always busy, responding to the needs and demands of the job.'

Aysen is quite cheerful about this. 'I enjoy it best,' she says, 'when there's plenty going on.'

Activity 6

Do you think that Aysen needs to manage her time better?

❐ YES   ❐ NO   ❐ MAYBE

Aysen does not have an obvious problem, as Kris the fire-fighter had. From what we know of her so far, it is hard to say whether she could manage her time more effectively. We would need to ask her:

What are your goals and objectives?

Are you achieving them?

As far as we can tell, Aysen is probably achieving her work objectives, but people who fill up their time with low-level tasks frequently neglect longer-term goals. Because they are so busy responding to the demands of the moment, they can miss opportunities.

Activity 7

Can you think of **two** longer-term goals that Aysen might possibly overlook?

_____

_____

_____

_____

Examples of goals Aysen might neglect are:

- staff training programme;
- improved staff morale;
- her own personal and/or professional development and possible promotion;
- improvements to the store.

These are examples of longer-term goals, because there will be no immediate results from actions Aysen might take in these areas.

So 'responding to demands' is likely to be another activity trap. Like crisis management, it can mean that all the time is used up on immediate tasks, and none is left for time management and planning. But, whereas Kris is engaged in bursts of frantic activity, probably followed by periods of recuperation, Aysen fills up her day with an endless round of fairly routine chores, many of them not difficult or not interesting. If Kris tries to plan, others will override his plans by imposing a series of jobs that cannot be postponed. Aysen should be planning, but may find it easy not to do so.

Activity 8 · 3 mins

Do you allow your days to be filled with routine tasks? ☐? YES ☐? NO

If you answered YES, write down any longer-term goals that you may well be neglecting because of this.

_____

_____

_____

_____

_____

_____

Writing down your longer-term goals is a good idea, because it helps to make them clearer in your mind.

6 Activity trap 3: the treadmill

Lisa is an office first line manager in the planning department of a local authority. The workload varies in a regular fashion, in five-week cycles. The final week of the cycle is very busy, but the pace of the work at other times is quite steady. The work which the office handles is fairly simple and repetitive, and Lisa sometimes envies people (like Kris the fire-fighter) who have an exciting time of it at work. Her own job, she says 'Is like being on a treadmill. You jog along every day, but you never seem to get anywhere. Some mornings it's an effort to get out of bed and come to work.'

Things may improve in the future, as the computerized filing system is being updated, but the planner in charge of the installation is over-worked and it is taking a long time.

Activity 9

Do you think Lisa could benefit from thinking how to manage her time?

☐ YES ☐ NO

How could we find the best way for Lisa to do so?

_____

_____

_____

_____

It seems likely that Lisa would benefit from thinking about how to manage her time. The situation isn't all that different from the previous one – 'Activity trap 2: responding to demands'. In both cases the person concerned is busy, without seeming to be making much progress. Lisa is rather worse off, because she isn't enjoying her job, and has much less variety.

People who feel their job is a treadmill are faced with an endless succession of uninspiring tasks. Work is not challenging but frustrating, and for this reason can be very stressful. The only way out of this activity trap is to look for new opportunities.

To help Lisa, we need to ask once again:

- What are your personal and professional goals?
- What stands in the way of achieving them?
- What opportunities are there?

Lisa may consider that there aren't enough opportunities available where she works and that the only way out is to find another job. The chances are, though, that there are possibilities within the same job that she has not explored. For example, she may be able to get involved in updating the filing system, to help bring the new procedures into operation more quickly.

Activity 10

You may well feel that your job is a treadmill and that you are working hard on dreary tasks, day after day. If you do, try to think of one opportunity you have to alter things.

_____

_____

_____

Is there anything that stands in the way of taking this opportunity?

_____

_____

_____

What can you do about it?

_____

_____

_____

If you are concerned about being on a treadmill, perhaps you might consider:

■ whether any training is available to you that will help you extend your range of skills and the type of work you could tackle;

■ formulating a plan for changing things, and talking to your manager about it;

■ getting your team together and holding an ideas or 'brainstorming' session, to try to come up with new ideas and approaches to the work.

People who feel they are working on treadmills generally don't enjoy their work. And people who don't enjoy their work are probably not doing either themselves or their employers justice.

7 Getting out of the trap

We have looked at three cases where people could manage their time better, and the problems associated with each case.

■ Crisis management. Main problems:

■ the crisis manager suffers from stress and fatigue;
■ mistakes are made in the job;
■ crises are expensive.

■ Responding to demands. Main problems:

■ longer-term goals may be overlooked;
■ opportunities may be missed.

■ The treadmill. Main problems:

■ stress through frustration;
■ opportunities may be missed.

Each of these cases provides an example of an activity trap.

When people fall into an activity trap, they spend most of their time responding to the next, or the most pressing, demand **without** thinking about what they are trying to achieve.

The hazard is that they may lose sight of their goals. And the result of doing that may be that they achieve nothing very much at all.

The way out of an activity trap is to:

set goals; choose priorities; make decisions.

We'll be looking at priorities and decisions in the next session.

Self-assessment 1

10 mins

1   Complete the following sentences with a suitable word or words, chosen from the list below.

 a Managing time means getting more _____ over how we spend our time and making sensible _____ about how we use it.
 b To become a crisis manager, simply do_____. A crisis will occur sooner or later.
 c Managing time means making the _____ _____ of your time.
 d The way out of an activity trap is to set _____: choose _____; make _____.

BEST	CONTROL	DECISIONS	DECISIONS
GOALS	NOTHING	PRIORITIES	USE

2   Pick out the **incorrect** statements from the list below.

 a Crises can be very costly to an organization.
 b Time management means dealing with the problems caused by overwork. It also means finding time to take advantage of available opportunities.
 c In order to manage time better, we need to think about what others would like us to achieve, and who stands in the way of us achieving it.
 d It is natural to try to avoid a crisis because nobody enjoys them.

3   Select the **two** statements from the list below which best describe the nature of activity traps.

Activity traps:

 a are routine ways of working from which there's no escape;
 b include firefighting, the treadmill and 'responding to demands';
 c can cause stress, frustration, errors and missed opportunities;
 d help us to recognize our goals.

4   All the incomplete words in the paragraph below begin with the letter 't'. What are they?

Managers and t_____ leaders are in danger of falling into activity t_____, one of which is the t_____, in which the person concerned faces an endless succession of routine t_____. To t_____ control of your t_____, you need to use t_____ designed to help you get out of these t_____. In the case of the t_____, t_____ may be the answer, as it could give you the skills to tackle more interesting t_____.

Answers to these questions can be found on page 97.

8 Summary

- **Managing time** means:

  - taking more control over how we spend our time;
  - making sensible decisions about the way we use it.

- When taking control and making decisions about how we spend our time, it's useful to distinguish between short-term **objectives** and longer-term **goals**, both at work and in your personal life.

- In order to manage time better, we need to ask:

  - what are we trying to achieve?
  - what stands in the way of achieving it?

- **Activity traps** include:

  - **crisis management**, in which those involved stagger from one crisis to the next. It is an expensive way of operating, causes stress and fatigue, and results in mistakes.
  - **responding to demands**, which results in days filled with a variety of jobs. Time is used up and it is very easy to put off planning activities.
  - **the treadmill**, an endless series of uninteresting tasks. Stress results from frustration and boredom, and opportunities may be missed.

- The way out of an activity trap is to

  - set goals;
  - choose priorities;
  - make decisions.

Session B
Deciding how to use time

 ## 1 Introduction

Most first line managers probably feel they have too many things to do. How is it possible to know how to apportion time appropriately? Is it best to do the easy things first, or the important things, or the urgent things? How can we decide?

In this session of the workbook, we'll start by looking at the decision process itself. Next, briefly, the subject will be 'timing' rather than 'time', for it's important to get the timing of a decision right.

We will then go on to examine the typical demands made on our time and who makes them.

After that the discussion turns to habits – good ones and bad ones.

The rest of this session is devoted to a clever device called a **time management grid**, which should help you decide just how urgent and important a particular job is.

2 Making decisions

The responsibility for making decisions is a key feature of management. But what do we really mean by a 'decision'?

Activity 11

How would you explain the word 'decision' to someone who hasn't heard it before?

_____

_____

_____

_____

A decision can be defined as:

■   a choice between options;
■   what happens when someone picks up one option rather than other options;
■   a selection of one thing, or a preference for one thing, over another.

When someone makes a decision, they are choosing between two or more options.

Why is this important to effective time management?

> 'More than any other time in history, mankind faces a cross-roads. One path leads to despair and utter hopelessness. The other, to total extinction. Let us pray we have the wisdom to choose correctly.' – Woody Allen.

The reason is that we all have choices about how to spend our time, so it's sensible to think about the process of selecting the best options.

As a manager, you will certainly be familiar with the decision-making process. You probably have to make decisions every hour of every day – big decisions and small decisions.

By analysing the way that decisions are made, it's possible to identify a series of stages in the process, although sometimes these stages are passed through so quickly we may be hardly aware of them.

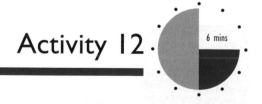

Activity 12

Suppose you are a first line manager in a warehouse. You've been instructed by your manager to keep overtime to an absolute minimum. On Thursday morning you are given a large order which you are told by the sales department must be picked and packed by Monday. You know you can't finish the job in time without overtime working. Your manager is away and won't be back until Friday.

You could organize some overtime for Thursday and Friday and risk your manager being annoyed that his instructions were ignored. Or you could leave a decision until he gets back and ask him to authorize weekend working. Weekend working would cost the company more money than weekday overtime.

One way or another you have to make a decision.

Jot down the **stages** by which you would come to a decision. **What** you decide isn't so important for the purposes of this exercise; it's the stages which your thinking would go through before you carried out your decision that we're interested in.

_____

_____

_____

_____

_____

_____

_____

_____

One way to list the stages of decision-making is shown below. Don't worry if you described a different approach – there are no hard-and-fast rules about this. The method described is a useful one, though.

- It is useful to begin by making sure you have all the correct information available. For the case described in the Activity, you might ask such questions as:

  - Do sales really need the order in full by Monday? Is a part shipment possible?
  - What exactly were the manager's instructions?
  - Are there members of your team available to work either on Thursday and Friday or at the weekend?
  - Is it possible to contact the manager?

  At this first stage we are gathering facts and making sure they're correct. A good name for this stage is the **knowledge** stage.

Tip: Defining your objectives is vital. If you aren't sure what your problem is, you'll be fortunate to solve it at all.

- Once you've gathered and checked all the information available, it's important to decide what exactly the problem is. We can call this the **objectives** stage. In it you are asking:

  - What am I trying to achieve?
    (We'll look at how to set objectives later in this session.)

- Next comes the **alternatives** stage. Here you are asking:

  - Given the facts available, and knowing what I'm trying to achieve, what are the choices open to me?

■ The next stage can be called the **look ahead** stage. The questions here are:

    ■ How would these alternatives work out?
    ■ How far would they go to meeting my objectives?
    ■ What would be the costs (financial and otherwise) of adopting each alternative?

■ The final stage is the **action** stage.

This is when you make a choice between your alternatives, put it into practice and see how it works out.

In summary, the stages of decision-making we have identified are:

K nowledge

O bjectives

A lternatives

L ook ahead

A ction

The initial letters of these stages spell the word KOALA. (A koala is the name of a small Australian marsupial that eats the leaves of eucalyptus trees.)

So much for the decision-making process. What about the timing of decisions?

Koalas aren't particularly known for their decisiveness, but they could be said to stick to their decisions. They sleep by curling up on the branches of trees, grasping them firmly with their feet, and will not release their grip, even when mortally wounded.

2.1 Timing it right

While this workbook is mostly concerned with the problem of saving and gaining time, doing things at the right time is also important.

The real-life manager is expected not only to reach the best possible decisions, but to implement them at the optimum moment. For instance:

■ The football manager has to consider whether to bring on substitute players early in the match, in the hope that they will liven up a team playing badly, or to wait in case someone gets injured.

■ A social worker may have to decide whether a child's parents will keep their promises, or whether their standards of care will fall once more. At what point – if ever – is it right to take that child away from its parents?

■ Certain kinds of crops (such as asparagus) must be harvested during very short critical periods of growth. Too early or too late, and the plant's value is greatly reduced.

Given all the relevant information, it may be possible to set rules or procedures by which the correct timing of a decision can be achieved. For example, a fixed number of days after printing out a bill, an office computer may be programmed to generate a reminder letter that payment is overdue.

Typically, however, the timing of a management decision will depend on the manager's judgement, based on the information available. We are back to the **knowledge** stage of our KOALA decision-making process, for:

to get your timing right, you have to base your decisions on the best information you can get.

Of course, if you are not in control of decisions about time, it probably means that:

- you are responding to the **demands** of others, or
- you are doing things out of **habit**.

Let's look at these two 'governors' of time more closely.

3 Identifying demands

Who makes demands on your time?

The following list is typical of the demands made on managers. See whether any of these apply to you, and then do Activity 13, which follows.

- Workteam members demand from you:

  - clear instructions about tasks;
  - training in new tasks;
  - discussion about any proposed changes;
  - that an interest be taken in them;
  - help with problems.

- Higher management demand that you:

  - lead your team effectively;
  - meet specific targets;
  - feed back information;
  - implement instructions.

■ Other teams demand that you:

- ■ work in unison with them, for the benefit of the organization;
- ■ share information.

■ Customers demand from you:

- ■ a quality product;
- ■ a professional service;
- ■ courtesy.

Activity 13

15 mins

The list above is a general one: not all the items may apply to you, and there may be many others that do. Think about who makes demands on **your** time, and what they expect from you. Write your thoughts in the space below.

Who makes the demand?	**What do they demand?**

In filling out the list above of the demands made on your time at work, you may also have been conscious of demands made on your time **outside** work – your home and social life. It is not always easy to separate the two.

It's not possible to respond to every demand. In a typical situation, you might be working with your team – perhaps giving them training – when a member of management turns up, wanting to talk to you. You can't do two things at once, so you have to decide which demand is the more important or the more pressing.

Sometimes, multiple demands can be met simply by meeting one demand followed by the other. For instance, if two members of your team want to talk to you privately, you can talk to them each in turn.

In other situations, demands may conflict, and it isn't so easy to deal with them. If you are trying to plan a detailed schedule which needs all your concentration and you are repeatedly interrupted, the detailed work may suffer.

Activity 14 · 3 mins

How do you **cope** with the problem of being interrupted? What do you do if:

■ you have an urgent and important task, and can't afford any interruptions?

_____

_____

_____

_____

■ you are trying to do something important, but know that other matters can't be neglected for very long?

_____

_____

_____

_____

you are being interrupted repeatedly with trivial demands?

_____

_____

_____

_____

We all have our methods for handling interruptions, or the threat of them. It may be possible to:

■ refuse them: try to say no;
■ postpone dealing with them: offer a later time when you will deal with the interruption;
■ minimize the interference: agree to give up a strictly limited amount of your time to the interruption;
■ avoid them.

When you know you must get some work done that will require all your concentration, I hope you agree that the best approach is to set aside a time and find a quiet place to work, and refuse all other requests at this time.

If you are very firm about this, most people will learn to leave you alone during this period. This method is especially effective if you always refuse to deal with interruptions either when you are in a certain place (such as in an office with the door shut) or at a regular time each day. We shall have more to say about habits like this later in this session.

This is also a good approach in the case where what you're doing is important, but you know that other matters can't be left for long. In such circumstances, you may be able to tell others to interrupt you only if certain events occur. For example, you might tell your team: 'I just have to get this report finished for the meeting tomorrow. I know what you're doing is important too, and if you really need me, give me a call. But I'd be grateful if you could try to cope until four o'clock.'

As for repeated trivial interruptions, it may be necessary to make clear that you won't tolerate them. There are many ways to say this, not all of them impolite.

Activity 15

Do you remember the types of activity traps we looked at in Session A? They were:

■ crisis management;
■ responding to demands;
■ the treadmill.

What kinds of demands are placed upon the first line managers in each of those cases? We have described the demands on the crisis manager to give you a start.

Crisis management

■ A large number of demands, of different kinds.
■ Most, or all, of the demands are said to be urgent and important.
■ Most, or all, of the demands seem to come from management.
■ The need for longer-term planning activities seems to be ignored.

Responding to demands

_____

_____

_____

_____

The treadmill

_____

_____

_____

_____

Answers to these questions can be found on page 100.

3.1 Thinking about objectives

The previous Activity stresses the fact that one of the main things to suffer when people have many demands on their time is the achievement of longer-term goals. It is all too easy to become like a ship with no one at the helm, blown first this way and then the other.

What can we do about this?

The first step is to identify **objectives**, then, once you have a clear idea of what you want to achieve, you can ask yourself two questions:

- which demands on my time are important to achieving my objectives?
- what else should I be doing, which no one is asking me to do?

Objectives aren't achieved simply by responding to the demands of others.

Most people would agree that, if you don't know where you are going, you won't know when you get there, and you won't be able to choose the best way of travelling. So when you carry out any sort of planning – whether it is reorganizing the railways or making a cup of tea – you need to have a clear idea of where you want to end up. In planning terms this idea is called an 'objective' or 'goal'.

Objectives vary in detail, depending on who is going to use them. This is illustrated in the diagram below.

At the very top of the objective tree there is often a mission statement which most organizations publish as an expression of their ideals and ambitions. For example, the mission of the University of Cambridge is 'To contribute to society through the pursuit of education, learning, and research at the highest international levels of excellence'.

Below the mission statement, objectives get more practical. There are three levels, each one covering the same area of activity as the one above it, but at a more detailed level. They are:

- organizational objectives;
- project (or team) objectives;
- task objectives.

Organizational objectives. These are general statements of the long-term goals of the whole organization. For example 'To provide an efficient service for all claimants at the benefits office' or 'To maintain all corporation parks and gardens to a high standard, for the benefit of the public'.

Project (or team) objectives. These are also general in subject matter but relate more to the medium term. They describe the goals set for a particular project or team, and will often have a time limit. Examples would be 'To train new call centre recruits in customer care' or 'To develop a new computer system to enable tennis court bookings to be made online'.

Task objectives. These are short-term and are more detailed than project or team objectives, being focused on specific tasks to be carried out within the project or team, for example 'Within the next 5 days, to write a piece of computer code that will allow a call centre operator to accurately record an electricity meter reading in the customer billing system'.

Finally, you will probably come across one other category of objectives – **performance objectives**. These are statements of personal goals set down for each member of the team or project, usually during a job review. They clarify what is expected of each person in terms of quality, standards of performance and personal development. Performance objectives are discussed in detail in another workbook, *Managing Performance*.

Activity 16 · 5 mins

Jot down the general longer-term objectives of your team. If they have never been written down, you may want to think about what they should be, A good starting point might be to write down what you think the team's overall function is.

_____

_____

_____

_____

_____

_____

It is important that you know your team objectives and can define them. If you aren't sure what they are, it may be a good idea to discuss the subject with your manager, or talk them over with your team.

The higher-level objectives are very general in the way they describe what has to be achieved, but they are not much help in getting a particular job done. So, if you are given the objective 'To develop a new computer program to enable tennis court bookings to be made online', you will not be any clearer about:

- what exactly you are expected to do;
- what standards you have to achieve;
- what your priorities should be;
- what resources will be needed (this covers everything from desks and pens, to people to do the job);
- what skills you will need;
- when it has to be completed.

So the bottom level of objectives (task objectives) have to be much more specific, with all these details agreed before any work can start.

3.2 Determining objectives

The first stage of building a framework that will support you and your team in using time effectively is to **determine the objectives** that affect everyone's working activity. Every organization has its goals, which in turn are translated into practical departmental, team and individual objectives. Every manager has a role in this process of translating organizational goals into achievable objectives.

Objectives are usually passed on through:

- team briefings or meetings;
- continuing discussions between managers and staff;
- appraisal or performance review.

Clear objectives will support your team members' understanding of what is expected of them.

Individuals and organizations will have their priorities. The organization's priorities will dictate where the business focus needs to lie. Everyone within the organization needs to recognize what these priorities are. Understanding business priorities and business needs helps to set objectives within realistic time frames. At the same time it will be clear that not all objectives at team and individual level can have equal importance, because of the organization's priorities. This is an area where conflicts may arise, and we will look at this problem in more detail in the final session of this workbook. A tool for helping to decide on your own priorities is discussed later in this session.

How do we create clear objectives? Objectives should be SMART:

Specific
Measurable
Achievable
Relevant
Time bound.

Let's look at how we can build these five aspects into our objectives.

Specific means that the objective should state what actions need to be carried out, using language that is easily understood by everyone concerned. For example, '*dress the front window every Friday*' is a specific statement for a sales assistant.

For an objective to be **measurable** it needs to be set in a way that allows for assessment. If there is no measurement attached to the objective, it will be difficult to decide when the objective has been achieved, where there has been a shortfall, or where requirements have been exceeded. '*Dress the front window every Friday, using at least two new stock items.*' If more than two new stock items are used the objective has been exceeded, if fewer then it has not been achieved.

Objectives need to be **achievable**, taking into account the resources – including people, materials, equipment, money, information and time – that are available both to the organization and to the individual. There is no point, for example, in giving a sales assistant the objective that he or she should '*Dress the front window every Friday, using at least two new stock items*', if they don't have the time or skills to do this. This doesn't mean, however, that you shouldn't set objectives that involve stretching an individual's capability.

For an objective to be **relevant** it needs to make sense to individuals in terms of their job roles. It must also support the overall objectives of the department and the business. If the business had most passing trade on a Saturday morning then the re-dressing of the window every Friday evening would be relevant. If the business was closed each weekend but had a lot of passing trade on Monday then the objective would still be relevant. However, if the business sold most of its goods on-line or by telephone, then the objective would have no apparent relevance.

Finally, objectives need to be **time bound**. Questions to consider include:

- By when must the objective be achieved?
- How much time is needed to achieve the objective?
- When will the objective be reviewed?

The first question is relatively straightforward in principle. A definite date and/or time deadline needs to be agreed and adhered to. For example, the objective that '*The window is to be dressed every Friday, between 5 pm and 6 pm*' is clearly time bound. It includes a deadline for completion (6 pm on Friday). It also includes an assumption, based on experience, that the task can be satisfactorily completed within an hour at the most.

This example was a simple one. However, where an objective is complex, and requires several different tasks and types of tasks in order to achieve it, then it is important that the process be **monitored** and that regular **review** points be agreed. Reviewing an objective only after the tasks involved have been completed will mean that opportunities will be missed for changing either the approach, or possibly the working methods. For example, if, as the work progresses, it becomes clear that part of the process isn't going as planned, or the deadline begins to seem unrealistic, then a new approach or target date may need to be negotiated. It is too late to make improvements at the end of the process. We'll look at tools for managing complex tasks in more detail in Session C.

By agreeing and setting SMART objectives for all team members we can:

- set out exactly what is needed;
- establish priorities, in line with organizational needs;
- define how successes can be measured;
- try and make sure that the necessary resources will be available, where and when needed;
- clarify the points in time when the objective can be considered and finalized.

Activity 17 · 4 mins

Which of the following do you think are good SMART objectives?

a To produce a set of accounts for P Hennessy Ltd by 31 May from records provided by them.
b To write a speech lasting 30 minutes for the Archery Club meeting next Saturday.
c By 31 August, to have sold 40 top-of-the-range washing machines from the York warehouse.
d To interview each member of the team in order to identify their current IT skills, and discuss any further training they would like to have.

c is the only effective SMART objective. It is specific, measurable, achievable, related to the job and has a clear time limit.

a is not measurable because it does not give enough information about the content, layout, etc, to know whether the accounts are of the required standard.

b is not sufficiently specific – it doesn't indicate the subject of the speech.

d does not contain a time limit for the task.

So objectives may be either general (relating to the overall organization, project or team) or specific (relating to the task).

In the case of an office supervisor, a general objective might have been 'To provide an efficient and effective clerical and administrative service to all departments', while one of the specific objectives might have been 'To ensure that 20,000 customer information packs are correctly prepared, checked and posted by Friday afternoon'.

Having clear objectives is necessary for good control.

If your line manager presents you with an overall general objective relating to a group of tasks to be carried out by you and your team, you will have to devise specific objectives for carrying out those tasks.

But you need your team members to 'buy in' to the idea, so the next step is to **negotiate** and agree each specific task objective with the member of your team who will carry it out. The result will be that he or she will take ownership of the task and feel responsible for making it succeed.

The purpose of negotiating is for you to make sure that the team member:

- is clear about his or her role;
- knows who is responsible for what;
- understands what the required standards are;
- feels able to meet the required standard;
- knows what resources are available;
- knows what the deadlines are;
- understands the order in which tasks are to be done;
- is motivated.

If you discuss all these points with your team members, you are giving them the opportunity to ask questions and mention anything they are worried about. Once all this has been discussed and agreed, everyone is much more likely to feel really involved.

Activity 18 · 20 mins

Select up to **two** objectives that you have agreed with members of your team. Do these objectives fulfil the SMART criteria as set out above? Rewrite these objectives, if necessary, as SMART objectives.

_____

_____

_____

_____

_____

_____

SMART objectives form the basis for planning the work that is needed, instead of just responding to demands.

3.3 Monitoring objectives

Where objectives have been set, performance must be monitored to ensure that the objectives have been achieved. That is why SMART objectives should be Measurable. To measure them, you need to collect data on performance. This could be quantitative data, such as units produced, sales made or applications processed. Equally, it could be simple observation of a job completed or a piece of equipment back on line.

The front line manager who goes round the work area several times a day and maintains a continuous contact with events builds up a great deal of useful information about the performance of the team and the achievement of objectives. By doing this, you can:

■ give guidance based on your greater knowledge and experience;
■ learn about problems and new ideas;
■ find out how the team's plans are progressing;
■ perhaps make minor adjustments and corrections to the plans so as to keep them on course.

This day-by-day, hour-by-hour interaction with the team is a normal and necessary part of supervision.

The process of comparison should be quite straightforward, provided that:

- work objectives are well defined;
- measurement of results is accurate.

Although there are no hard and fast rules to be applied, the two key points to be borne in mind when judging performance against objectives are that:

- everything you do takes up time, so you don't want to check anything unnecessarily frequently;
- you need to assess performance well before it becomes too late to take corrective action,

The main point to remember is that the cost and effort of monitoring has to be balanced against the benefits of knowing exactly how well your objectives have been met.

Now let's turn our attention from objectives to habits.

4 Habits

Habits are routines – repeated patterns of behaviour.

Habits can be necessary and useful, but they can also work against your interests.

4.1 Getting into bad habits

Read the following two cases:

> Delroy's company sold agricultural equipment, and Delroy's job was to run short training courses on the use and upkeep of the equipment. When a new piece of machinery came out – about every three years – Delroy had to learn about it himself. During the first few courses a lot of questions would arise and Delroy sometimes had to go back to the manufacturer for the answers. Then, after a while, he would get to know the equipment well, and could usually answer any questions. His training tended to develop into a pattern, which was repeated week after week.
>
> One day Delroy was called into his manager's office. 'I've had complaints, Delroy, that your sessions are boring and that you look bored yourself. How can we expect our customers to be enthusiastic if we aren't?'

Riaz was a nursing team leader in a clinic. He took his job very seriously and hardly ever took time off. When he did he would make sure his staff knew where he was at all times, and told them to call him if anything difficult came up. His team members got into the habit of calling Riaz whenever they were in the least bit unsure about how to deal with a problem. Then one day Riaz went sick himself. While he was recovering, he fretted and worried about the job and was amazed (and secretly rather disappointed) to find out that the rest of the staff had coped quite well without him. Riaz's doctor told him that he must relax more if he didn't want to become ill again. After that, Riaz decided to break old habits and take a completely different approach to his job.

Activity 19

3 mins

What do these cases have in common?

_____

_____

_____

_____

_____

_____

_____

_____

It seems that, in these cases, the people concerned got into the habit of working in a particular way without thinking too much about the consequences, either for themselves or others.

- Delroy got into the habit of training in the same way over and over again, without thinking of the effects on himself or his audience. He filled his days without enjoying what he was doing.
- Riaz got into the habit of being obsessed with his job and of persuading himself that he was indispensable, without thinking of the effects on himself and his team. He filled his whole life with work.

Habits can get in the way when:

- they lead us to do things which are not important to the job, or to waste time;
- they do not help us to achieve our goals and objectives;
- they do not help us to fit in properly with the people we need to work with.

In summary:

bad habits may result in time that is poorly used.

4.2 Useful habits

This is a big year for Cardchester: it is celebrating its 900th anniversary. To commemorate the event, the city is presenting a festival, that will incorporate literary and musical events and other cultural highlights.

Reporting to the Director of Leisure Services, Bill Heldman has been appointed to oversee the organizing of the festival. It's a big job, and Bill knows he will have a hectic six-month period of preparation. He has a small team of assistants to help him with the seemingly endless list of tasks. However, Bill has resigned himself to the inevitable fact that he must be the main focal point for all activities. Everyone connected to the project will want to talk with him.

From past experience, Bill has learned that, in this kind of situation, the routine organizing and co-ordinating work will tend to dominate his time. What he knows he must keep track of is the 'big picture' — the overall plan of things. He has therefore set up a routine.

1 He meets his team at 8 am every morning, when they can expect fewest interruptions.

2 Incoming and outgoing calls are dealt with from 9 am to 11 am, and 4 pm onwards.

3 All face-to-face meetings and site visits are arranged during the afternoon, and Bill tries to get them over by 4 pm.

4 He makes it clear to everyone that he will be unavailable from 11 to 12 o'clock each day. During that hour, Bill shuts his office door, puts the answer-phone on, and sticks up a sign on the door saying: 'Bill Heldman is unavailable until 12 o'clock'. His answerphone message says: 'This is Bill Heldman. Thank you for calling. If you want to contact me, the best way is by fax or e-mail. My fax number is — — —, and my e-mail address is — — —'.

> What Bill does during his 'quiet hour' is simply thinking and planning. He resists any temptation to make any calls, and tries to examine the scheme from every conceivable point of view.

When we form the habit of doing certain things at certain times, others will come to expect that behaviour from us and so fit into **our** pattern of behaviour.

In this case, Bill also makes sure he sets aside a period every day, which he devotes to planning.

Although Bill has fixed habits, he's not an inflexible person. He is simply putting his experience to good use, for he knows that by setting up a daily pattern of working, he is more likely to achieve his objectives. He is in effect also making the statement: 'I want to be in control of my own time; I don't want to be buffeted along by events, or at the beck and call of everyone.'

Bill's story is an example of the fact that:

good habits can help people use time well.

We have seen that habits can be helpful or unhelpful in managing time. It can be useful to think about the things you do out of habit, and ask yourself three questions:

- What goal or objective is this habit helping me to achieve?
- How is it helping me to get my work done?
- How does the habit fit in with the people who make demands on my time?

Activity 20

Write down all your activities for a typical day that are done regularly, or out of habit. You can either do this from memory, or record everything you do for a particular work day; if you choose the latter, the list will obviously take you longer to complete.

Identify whether each routine is being done as the result of a demand, or as a consequence of a decision you have made. Then answer the question: 'What goal or objective is this habit helping me to reach?' Finally, decide whether each of your habitual activities is useful in helping you to get your work done.

Time start	Demand/ my decision?	Habitual work activity	Helping me reach the goal/objective of:	Useful? YES/NO

If you are planning to use your responses for your S/NVQ portfolio, you should now take it to the next stage and decide how you will alter your daily routine to (a) eliminate habits that are not useful, and (b) put habits in place that will help you achieve your goals and objectives.

Most of us do lots of things out of habit, without thinking why we do them or whether they are useful. It helps sometimes to analyse what we do, and to try to think of ways of organizing our day better.

One good habit is to spend time each day sorting out your priorities.

5 Priorities

What makes something a priority? What are the different types of priority?

Activity 21

2 mins

What is meant when something is described as 'high priority?'

_____

_____

_____

_____

_____

When you hear the phrase 'high priority' or 'top priority' mentioned, it may mean that the task or required action:

- is very urgent and must be dealt with immediately;
- is very important and should be given a great deal of attention and thought;
- is both urgent and important: it must be done immediately and done well;
- takes precedence over everything else.

Check that your answer is along the lines of one of these.

You will notice that we used the words 'urgent' and 'important' in our answer. Let's now think about the difference between these two words.

Activity 22

3 mins

What do these words mean? Write down your own definitions of the two words:

Something is urgent when _____

_____

_____

Something is important when _____

_____

_____

These words are often confused, even though they mean quite different things.

5.1 Urgency

Something is **urgent** when it demands immediate attention.

We can talk about things being more urgent or less urgent. When a job has to be done by a certain time, it becomes more urgent as the deadline draws near.

An urgent matter becomes more urgent as time passes.

Suppose Hensa, a first line manager, has two tasks:

■ to summarize the weekly timesheets of her workteam members, so that her manager can look at them next Monday morning;
■ to plan a new training programme for the following month.

Whatever the relative importance of the two tasks, the timesheet summary is more urgent, because the deadline is closer. We can show this on a vertical scale like this:

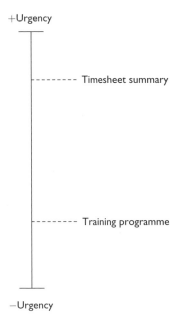

As time passes, both tasks will tend to become more urgent, and so should be moved up the chart.

5.2 Importance

Something is **important** when it has considerable significance or consequence.

You will note that this definition does not mention time.

The importance of a matter is not affected by the passing of time.

However, its importance may be affected by other things, which we discuss later in this session.

Referring back to the example of Hensa's two tasks, the timesheet summary is relatively unimportant, even though it is more urgent. The training programme is very important, even though it is not at all urgent.

We can use a horizontal scale to plot these two items:

−Importance   +Importance

Activity 23

Write down **three** jobs you know you will have to work on during the next week:

1 _____

2 _____

3 _____

List these jobs in order of urgency:

1 _____

2 _____

3 _____

Now list them in order of importance:

I   _____

2   _____

3   _____

It would be surprising if the order were the same in both cases. It is more usual for the order, in terms both of urgency and importance, to be different.

6 The time management grid

If we combine the two scales of urgency and importance, we get a grid, like this:

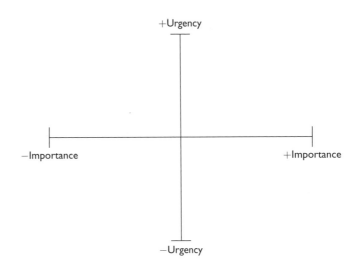

This is the time management grid.

It is now possible to be more precise about what we mean by a 'priority'. We can show on this grid the two tasks Hensa was considering – the timesheet summary and the training programme.

In the next figure, the timesheet summary is marked as 'I' and the training programme is marked as '2'.

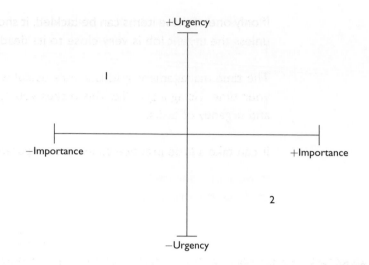

Really one of these tasks can be tackled, it should be the one unless one of the jobs is very close to its deadline.

The time management grid is useful because it can help you to think about how important each task is, and how urgent it is.

Activity 24 · 3 mins

How does the time management grid help? What do we gain from thinking about these two tasks in this way? Jot down two suggestions in the space below.

_____

_____

_____

_____

_____

_____

_____

_____

_____

_____

We are reminded that:

■ the timesheet summary is more urgent than the training programme, so it must be completed sooner;

■ the training programme is more important than the timesheet summary, so it probably deserves more attention and thought;

If only one of these items can be tackled, it should be the more important job, unless the urgent job is very close to its deadline.

The time management grid is a very useful way of looking at demands upon your time. Using a grid like this makes you consider the relative importance and urgency of tasks.

It can take a little practice to learn to separate urgency and importance.

Activity 25

A job has been lying on your desk for a week. When it first came in, you decided to enter it on the first point of the grid below. You had more important things to do and so the job is still outstanding. Now it has to be done before lunchtime. How could you plot the job's progress on the grid?

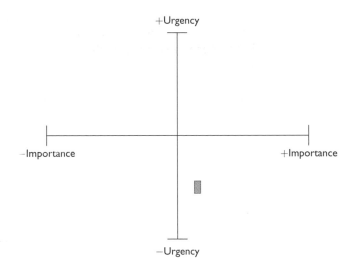

The answer to this question can be found on page 100.

Activity 26

What makes things more important?

Here is the time management grid again, with one job entered, moving to the right of the grid.

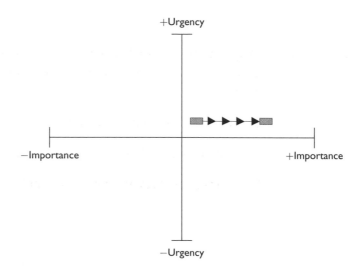

Using your experience, jot down **one** reason why a job could become more important.

_____

_____

_____

_____

There may be any number of reasons why a job will become more important. Some possible reasons are that:

■ your manager tells you it is important;

■ a new customer promises to place more orders if this job is of the highest quality;

■ it is decided that a report you are preparing will now be presented to senior management;

■ if a certain project is successful, your team will receive a special award.

A job changes in importance if its likely outcome changes.

But who decides how important a task is?

Activity 27

Suppose you have two jobs which are important. Your manager is emphasizing the importance of briefing your team for a visit of 'VIPs' next week. A team member is saying that he has an important matter he wants to discuss with you.

Who decides which is the more important task?

_____

Only **you** can decide. If it comes to a choice, you have to weigh up the effects of doing or not doing each task and make up your mind which one is more important.

This is true of everything you do.

Only you can decide how to respond to demands on your time.

Of course, this does not mean you can ignore other people.

Activity 28

You have planned to spend some time today training two new members of your team. Your manager asks you to take on another job, which you think is less important. Again, it's your decision, but you may want to take account of the demand that your manager is making – you might become rather unpopular if you ignored it. Without thinking through the consequences, list three options available to you.

_____

_____

_____

_____

_____

The following options are all possible:

■ Tell your manager that you haven't time – that the training is urgent and important.

■ Discuss with your manager your plans for training, and point out the effects of postponing them.

■ Tell your manager why you think the training is more important, but, if your manager insists that the other job must be done today, get him or her to agree a time when you will do the training without interruption.

■ Agree to your manager's request, without discussion.

■ Agree to your manager's request at the time, but arrange to have a meeting with him or her later, to discuss priorities.

> Many organizations now recognize the benefits of allowing individuals and groups the freedom to make their own decisions about the way they organize their work and their time. The term most commonly used for this is **empowerment.**

You may have thought of some other possible actions. Having listed the options, you have to make a decision. What you decide will depend on the knowledge you have – of the particular circumstances, your manager's likely reactions, and so on – and what you want to achieve. You must look ahead and try to determine what the effects of each option might be.

Working in an organization means you have to consider other people, and to play your part in trying to reach the organization's strategic goals. Often, your options will be constrained by this. You will seldom be able to make a decision about how to use your time without affecting others; sometimes it will be difficult to avoid creating a new problem for yourself as a result. But that doesn't mean that you should allow other people to control your time by making your decisions for you.

If the boss, or a customer, makes a demand or request, you may feel that you have no alternative but to go along with it. Nevertheless, you always do have options. The question is always: what's the best of these options, after taking into account your objectives and those of your organization? There's a world of difference in attitude between blindly doing what you're told or asked, and making your own decision after taking all factors into account. You're a manager: for the good of yourself and your employers, it's important to stay in control of your own decisions about what to do with your time.

We'll have more to say about this in the next session.

7 The quadrants

As you know, the time management grid is made up of four squares; another name for them is **quadrants**. By plotting tasks in a particular quadrant, we are categorizing them. This will help us to highlight certain dangers or risks.

Let us look at each of these quadrants in turn and identify the dangers.

7.1 The top right-hand quadrant

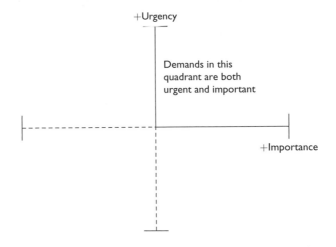

Tasks which fit into this quadrant get done, on the whole. The danger is:

tasks which are both urgent and important may not get done very well.

This is because they may be done in a hurry, as they are close to a deadline. So they may not get the time and care they deserve.

The top right-hand quadrant is the **high priority square**. There is sometimes a fine line between a high priority and a full-blown crisis.

7.2 The bottom right-hand quadrant

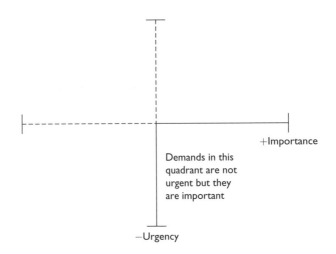

There are two types of task in this quadrant:

- tasks which have a deadline that is a long way into the future;
- tasks which do not have a deadline at all.

Activity 29

What do you think is the main risk applying to tasks in this category?

_____

_____

_____

_____

_____

The danger to tasks in this quadrant is that they may not get done at all.

Tasks which are not urgent may never get done.

Unless action is taken, tasks in this quadrant that have deadlines will rise into the priority square.

People who suffer from the frustrations of the treadmill usually have a number of tasks at the bottom of this quadrant, most of which don't have deadlines, and many of which they may never get around to doing.

Good time managers spend a lot of time dealing with items in this square.

Activity 30

Why do you think this is? What kind of tasks may be very important, yet not very urgent?

_____

_____

_____

_____

_____

The kind of tasks which tend to be very important and yet not urgent are the planning and longer-term tasks. That's why good time managers spend so much time there. We can call this square the **planning square.**

7.3 The top left-hand quadrant

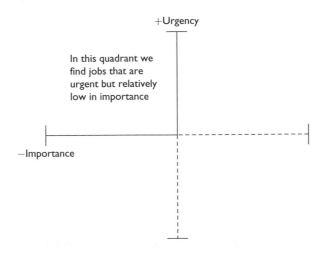

These things tend to get done – because they are urgent. The danger is that:

too much time may be spent on jobs which are urgent but not important.

This is time which we should spend on the more important jobs. Demands in this square should be dealt with quickly. A good name for this square is the **quick and simple square.**

7.4 The bottom left-hand quadrant

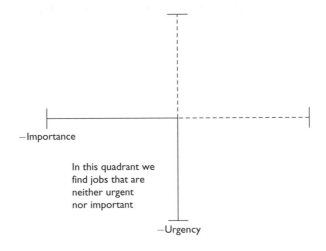

The danger here is that we spend time doing these things.

Activity 31

Why do we tend to spend time on things which are low in urgency **and** low in importance?

_____

_____

_____

_____

Generally, these things get done because they are easy. We may spend time on them simply because they **are** easy, or perhaps more enjoyable than other tasks we know we should be doing.

> 'What is this life if, full of care, We have no time to stand and stare?' – W.H. Davies, _Songs of Joy_.

Until a task in this square becomes more urgent, we may waste our time bothering with it. That's why we can call the bottom left-hand quadrant the **waste square.**

If a task has no urgency or importance, should you be doing it at all?

Of course, it depends on how you categorize your activities, and plot them on the grid. You might, for example, have a few tasks that you feel don't deserve to get into the planning square, because they aren't very important: tasks like tidying up your desk, 'housekeeping' your computer, or removing out-of-date notices from the notice-board, for example. Nevertheless, they need to be done, and are not a waste of time.

As you may have noticed, the names for our squares only give a rough indication of the kind of tasks that they are likely to contain.

7.5 The complete grid

Putting in these new names, our grid now looks like this:

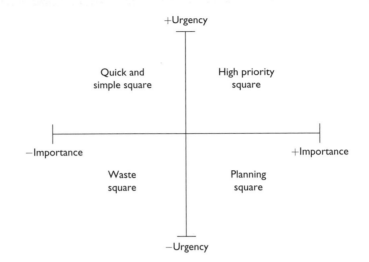

Activity 32 · 15 mins

In Activity 23 on page 38, you should have listed three jobs in order of urgency and importance. Now give some more thought to your outstanding workload, and write down **up to ten** tasks which you expect to have to face shortly. Instead of simply listing them, try to slot them into the four categories or quadrants of the management grid.

These jobs should be quick and simple:	These have reached high priority:
These have low urgency and importance:	**These are planning tasks:**

Self-assessment 2

10 mins

1   What are the stages of decision making?

     K_____

     O_____

     Alternatives

     L_____ _____

     A_____

2   Fill in the blanks in the following sentences with suitable words or phrases, chosen from the list below.

    a Using time badly may be caused by bad _____; good habits can help people _____.

    b There is a _____ that tasks that are _____ may take up too much time.

    c If its _____ change, a task may _____ in importance.

    d Only you can _____ how to _____ on your time.

    e You won't _____ if you simply respond to the demands of others.

    f If a task is _____, it may never get done at all.

    g Question: should you use your _____ on tasks that have _____?

    h The correct _____ depends on getting the best _____ you can.

    i The danger is that tasks which are _____ may not get done very well.

    j The _____ has no effect on the importance of something.

    EFFECTS OR RESULTS – DECIDE – DANGER – CHANGE –
    BOTH URGENT AND IMPORTANT – INFORMATION –
    ACHIEVE YOUR OBJECTIVES – PASSING OF TIME –
    NOT URGENT – NO URGENCY OR IMPORTANCE –
    HABITS – USE TIME WELL – URGENT BUT NOT IMPORTANT –
    TIMING OF A DECISION – TIME – RESPOND TO DEMANDS

3   The four quadrants of the time management grid can be labelled

HIGH PRIORITY SQUARE.
WASTE SQUARE.
QUICK AND SIMPLE SQUARE.
PLANNING SQUARE.

Place these names in the correct quadrants in the figure:

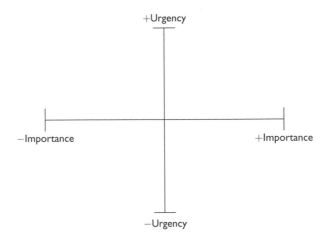

4   In the following grid, four jobs are shown. Originally, the jobs were placed in positions A1, B1, C1 and D1 on the grid. Later, they were all reassigned to new positions, labelled A2, B2, C2 and D2 respectively.

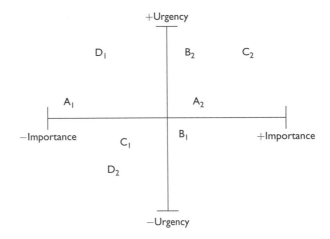

Say which of the four jobs best matches the description, in each case:

a A job which is nearing its deadline. A/B/C/D
b A job which has suddenly become more important, because of a management decision. A/B/C/D
c A job which was never very important, but now is hardly worth doing at all, because of a change of priorities. A/B/C/D
d A job which has increased dramatically, both in urgency and importance. A/B/C/D

Answers to these questions can be found on page 98.

8 Summary

- The **stages** of the decision-making process can be named as:

  K nowledge

  O bjectives

  A lternatives

  L ooking ahead

  A ction

- To get your **timing** right, you have to base your decisions on the best information you can get.

- Objectives aren't achieved simply by responding to the **demands** of others.

- Objectives need to be SMART

  Specific
  Measurable
  Achievable
  Relevant
  Time bound

- Performance against your objectives should be monitored.

- The cost and effort of monitoring needs to be balanced against the benefits of knowing your objectives have been met.

- Bad **habits** may result in time that is poorly used; good habits can help people use time well.

- Something is **urgent** when it demands immediate attention; an urgent matter becomes more urgent as time passes.

- Something is **important** when it has considerable significance or consequence; the importance of a matter is not affected by the passing of time.

- A job changes in importance if its likely **outcome** changes.

- Only **you** can decide how to respond to demands on your time.

- Tasks which are both **urgent and important** may not get done very well.

- Tasks which are **not urgent** may never get done.

- Too much time may be spent on jobs which are **urgent but not important**.

- If a task has **no urgency or importance**, you may need to question whether you should be doing it at all.

- A **time management grid** helps to decide **priorities**. The quick names for the management grid are: the high priority square, the waste square, the quick and simple square, and the planning square.

Session C
Making time work

■ 1 Introduction

You may often be 'working against time'. Why not recruit your enemy, and get time to work for you?

How can this be done? In principle, it's very easy: all you have to do is to analyse how you've spent your time in the past, then think ahead and plan what you want to do in the future. Then time falls into line; this precious resource becomes your friend and you can do with it what you will.

It is true that plans seldom survive reality completely intact: they are invariably made with insufficient knowledge for them to be carried through without a hitch. But, as we will discuss in this session of the workbook, it is still very important and useful to make plans. What you also must do is to be ready to adapt your plans to changing circumstances.

The way the session progresses is as follows. We start with a discussion about time logs, which analyse how you've previously spent your time. Then we go into the list system, which helps you plan how to spend your time in the future. We also introduce a useful tool for managing complex tasks in the most efficient way: the Gantt chart.

■ 2 Time logs

There are various ways of making a time log, and we'll look at these in turn.

2.1 Simple time logs

A simple time log is just a piece of paper on which you note everything you do in the course of the day, and the amount of time you spend doing it.

You need to use a fresh piece of paper for each day and keep the sheets in a file or folder so that you can refer to them easily when necessary. The log should be quite detailed and accurate.

2.2 Preprinted forms as time logs

There are a number of different formats for more complex time logs using preprinted forms. There is an example below. It includes space for: a daily plan, activities, the purpose of the activities, time taken on them and whether or not they were planned. It also includes a space to be filled in about achievements, problems and suggested actions to deal with problems.

Day Date Page No.	Plan		
Time	Activity	Tick if planned	Purpose
Achieved: (apart from planned items)			
Problems:			
Actions:			

Activity 33

Think for a few minutes about the advantages of keeping a time log. Then think about the difficulties. Write your ideas in the space below.

Advantages

_____

_____

_____

_____

Difficulties

_____

_____

_____

_____

The advantages may be that you have an accurate record of how you have used your time. This can help you in:

- better planning;
- identifying areas of waste;
- presenting a case to your manager about waste, the workload or other problems.

The difficulties may be that:

- it takes time to fill in the log;
- it is an extra chore to do;
- you will need to keep it going throughout the day. You will need to note what you're doing either continuously or at hourly intervals, because otherwise you will forget what you have done and the log will not be accurate.

If you think that the advantages apply to you and that you can overcome the difficulties, it is worth trying to keep a time log. Keep a log for two weeks or for a month, and then look up where all your time has gone.

2.3 Time logs for specific purposes

These are used for particular projects or problems, to keep track of waste or to help with planning. You may keep one, for example, to account for the amount of time wasted through a particular kind of problem – such as a printer breakdown – or on a specific project like a move to a different office.

Because they are not as comprehensive as other types of time log, specific logs are easier to keep. They may prove invaluable in understanding how your time is spent and in explaining this to others.

You may want to think about whether time logs might be a useful way of helping you and your team members keep track of how they use their time. They can be a valuable source of information about how long things really take.

A log is fine for analysing how you spent your time in the past. But if you want to decide how to spend your time in the future, you will need to use a different recording system.

3 Planning time for you and your team

To make the best use of your time you are going to have to do some forward thinking or planning. Two of the basic tools of the good time manager are:

- a **diary**;
- the **list system**.

You probably use at least one of these already, but you may require both. They are particularly helpful if you are in a job where there are a number of different demands upon your time.

Some obvious symptoms of bad time management are missed appointments, broken promises and things which simply have not been done. A diary and the list system will both help you avoid such problems.

3.1 Diaries

A **diary** is for long-range planning: to note appointments and commitments for weeks and months ahead. It will depend on your particular job as to whether you need to do this.

A **team diary** can be a very valuable means of agreeing and illustrating events that are relevant and important for all team members. The diary might show:

- dates and times of team meetings;
- scheduling requirements to meet customer orders;
- holiday periods for individual team members;
- parental leave for individual team members;
- training courses, for individuals or the full team.

Another way of illustrating this type of information is on a wall chart. The key point is that time-related information that will affect all team members needs to be readily available and accessible to everyone.

4 The list system

The **list system** can help you plan on a week-by-week, day-by-day basis. It is generally best to get into the habit of making a daily list at a particular time each day. First thing in the morning, or last thing at the end of the shift, are good times.

The list system consists of three steps:

- Step 1 Write down a list of all the things you want to do (that day, say).
- Step 2 Decide in what order you will tackle the items on the list.
- Step 3 Decide how long you will spend on each item.

Before we look more closely at these steps, let us consider who is most likely to gain from using the list system.

Activity 34

What kind of people are likely to benefit most from the list system?

_____

_____

_____

_____

_____

Some of those who might find the list system helpful are shown below; you may have thought of others.

- **Someone in charge of a general duties team**, which tackles a number of different tasks, is particularly likely to gain. If the workteam tends to carry out the same kind of tasks every day, less planning may be needed.
- **Those who have to communicate with a large number of people** as part of their job will find the system useful. The list can be used as a way of reminding them of matters which have to be taken up with each person.
- **People who are involved in any long-range or complex projects** can benefit, by listing the next actions to be taken.
- **Managers who have poor memories** can use a list to remind themselves of all the jobs they have outstanding. Even if you have a good memory, a list can reduce the burden of having to remember things – on top of everything else.

Now we'll look at the three steps of the list system.

4.1 Compiling your list

Tip: Try not to arrange appointments (for example, a mid-morning meeting) at such a time that it will be difficult to fit other events around it.

In Step I, you note down a list of all the things you want to do during a particular time period, for example, in one day or perhaps one week.

You may feel there's no point in listing events that will happen anyway, and which you can't do much about, or things which you always do every day. But you'll have to plan around these, so it's best to include them. The safest thing is to write down everything you can think of.

4.2 Order planning

Step 2 of the list system is deciding in what order you plan to tackle the items on your list.

The first thing to do is to identify those tasks that have a deadline.

■ Some items may have a **fixed deadline** – they must be completed by a certain time.

■ Others may have a **natural deadline**, in that they need to be done before another action can be taken. For instance, if you want a member of your workteam to do a different job from the usual one that day, you have to let that person know before work starts.

The next thing to do is to take the rest of the items on your list – those without a deadline – and plot them on a time management grid.

Activity 35 · 2 mins

How will this help?

_____

_____

_____

_____

_____

_____

Plotting your planned tasks on a time management grid will help you decide their relative importance and urgency. These decisions are not always easy, but they have to be taken.

If we miss out this stage, we may be tempted to 'plough into' the list without thought of what is important or urgent. The tendency in that case is to tackle the easy or pleasant tasks before the difficult or messy ones.

Here's an example.

Tracy, a team leader, makes a list at the end of the day, of all the tasks she would like to get done the following day. It looks like this:

	Task	Comment	Estimate
1	Write up the weekly report, so Declan can have it by 4 o'clock.	Must be done by 4 o'clock.	
2	Talk to Nasrim about the special purchase order for Whiteley and find out what it's about, so the team can be prepared to start on it early next week.		
3	Meeting of team leaders 2:30.	Fixed time: 2:30.	
4	Brief the team on the new fire regulations.		
5	Get in touch with the wages department about Julie's query – must be done before they close the weekly wage accounts at 1 o'clock.	Must be done before 1 o' clock.	
6	Tell Judah about the fault on his machine first thing.	Must be done first thing.	
7	Telephone June Crowthorne about the Sports Club Committee meeting.		
8	Continue planning the new floor layout with Teresa and Wendy.		
9	Check the documents on that Polish order before it goes out.	Must be done before the Polish order goes out.	
10	Spend some time with Marge during the day – probably need to see her twice for half an hour each.		

Note that the tasks, although numbered, have been jotted down in no particular order of priority.

(The last column will be filled in later.)

In the second column, Tracy has listed the jobs with a deadline or fixed time. We can arrange them in time order:

6   Must be done first thing.

5   Must be done before 1 o'clock.

3   Meeting of team leaders 2:30.

1   Must be done by 4 o'clock.

9   Must be done before the Polish order goes out.

From this she can see that the first job to be done in the morning is Job 6: tell Judah about the fault on his machine. Jobs 5, 3, 1 and 9 all also have fixed times or deadlines.

Now Tracy plots the remaining jobs without fixed deadlines or times on the time management grid:

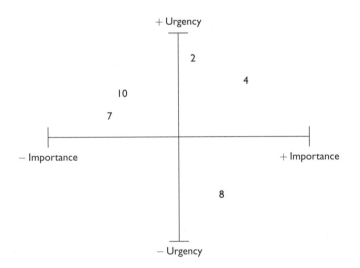

But there's some information still needed, before Tracy can draw up a timetable of events. She must estimate how long each job will take.

4.3 Allocating time

Step 3 in the list system is deciding how long you and your team members will spend on each item.

Activity 36 ·

When making out a list of things to do, do you think it might be better to estimate the time to be spent on each item **before** putting them in sequence, or the other way round?

_____

_____

Neither method is incorrect. The truth is that **both** the sequence and the amount of time to be spent have to be considered, when using the list system.

It's a good idea to think first about the sequence, because this prompts you to contemplate the importance of each task. The decisions you make about importance depend on the objectives you have in mind. But you also need to take into account the amount of time each task will take before making a final decision on what you are going to do.

When you have finished your planning, you will have a list of things you want to do, and the amount of time each is likely to take. You may well discover that, according to your estimates, you have 14 hours of work to complete in an eight-hour day! If that's the case you have at least learned that you won't get through your list without help.

Activity 37 ·

Suppose you are working on something that you think will take two hours to complete. As you reach the end of that time, you realize that it is going to take you two **more** hours to finish. What do you do in this situation? Write one suggestion in the space below.

_____

_____

_____

_____

What you must do is to consider which is more important: finishing the task or leaving it for the time being, and taking care of some of the other things you had planned to do.

It can be frustrating to have to leave a job unfinished. But you must remember to think about what will not get done if you stick with this job. Is there anything more important or more urgent? Is there anything you could get someone else in your team to do?

Now let's return to Tracy's list.

Tracy now fills in the third column – the estimates of the time taken to carry out each task:

		Task	Comment	Estimate
1		Write up the weekly report, so Declan can have it by 4 o'clock.	Must be done by 4 o'clock.	Half an hour.
2		Talk to Nasrim about the special purchase order for Whiteley and find out what it's about, so the team can be prepared to start on it early next week.		Talk max. 20 minutes, then preparation, up to 2 hours more.
3		Meeting of team leaders 2:30.	Fixed time: 2:30.	Hour and a half.
4		Brief the team on the new fire regulations.		20 minutes.
5		Get in touch with the wages department about Julie's query – must be done before they close the weekly wage accounts at 1 o'clock.	Must be done before 1 o'clock.	10 minutes.
6		Tell Judah about the fault on his machine first thing.	Must be done first thing.	10 minutes.
7		Telephone June Crowthorn about the Sports Club Committee meeting.		10 minutes.
8		Continue planning the new floor layout with Teresa and Wendy.		Several hours yet, probably.
9		Check the documents on that Polish order before it goes out.	Must be done before the Polish order goes out.	Allow an hour.
10		Spend some time with Marge during the day – probably need to see her twice for half an hour each.		Total 1 hour.

Let's remind ourselves of the items without deadlines that Tracy plotted on the time management grid:

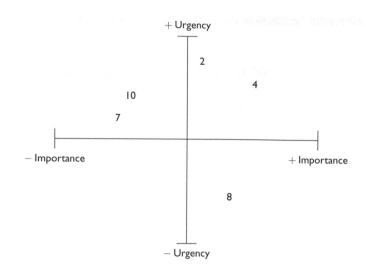

So, now she can get down to her day plan, which looks like this:

	Task	*Planned time*
6	Must be done first thing.	say 9:00 to 9:15
5	Won't take long – may as well do that next.	say 9:15 to 9:30
9	The Polish order documents are urgent – it's probably best to get these out of the way, in case I miss it.	9:30 to 10:30
4	These new fire regulations: it's the most important job.	10:30 to 10:50
10	Must try to talk to Marge.	10:50 to 11:20
2	I'll arrange to see Nasrim at 11:30 and then spend some time on the preparation. The rest will have to be done tomorrow.	11:30 to lunchtime
	Lunch	1:00 to 2:00 pm
1	Straight after lunch, I'll do Declan's report.	2:00 to 2:30
3	Meeting of team leaders.	2:30 to 4:00
8	Must get in some time with Teresa and Wendy on the floor planning.	4:00 to 4:30
10	See Marge again before she goes home.	4:30 to 5:00

Tracy notes: 'I didn't list Job 9 – have to find ten minutes to phone June about the Sports Club meeting. I know it isn't that important, so if I don't find time it'll have to wait.'

Activity 38 ·

3 mins

What comments, if any, would you make about Tracy's day plan?

_____

_____

_____

The one comment we would make is that she is cutting things a bit fine. If she gets one lengthy interruption or unexpected event, she will lose track of her schedule, and this may cause inconvenience to other people as well as herself.

So – she should mark the less important jobs, so that she does not find herself doing those at the expense of the more important ones. For instance, if the team leaders' meeting is running a bit late, the discussion with Marge may have to give way to the planning meeting.

5 Gantt charts

A Gantt chart is, in simple terms, a visual plan of a complex job. Gantt charts are most commonly used in project planning and project management, because they are a practical means of setting out, in a straightforward and visual way, what needs to be done and when. They can be used to manage both your own time and that of your team members.

When preparing a Gantt chart you will need to:

■ **break the job down** into smaller tasks;
■ **gather all the relevant information** in relation to the job, including people required and resource availability – including time;
■ **place the tasks in order** – that is, decide what needs to be completed before another task can begin;
■ **allocate the necessary resources** to each task.

Breaking the job down into smaller tasks may seem a bit daunting at first. But as a general rule, the job can most usefully be divided up into quite general tasks, and then, as we shall see below, each of these can be divided into more specific tasks at a later date. Let's look at a simple example to see how it works.

- Anton manages events for a company of accountants. A major meeting is being held for 50 participants, and he has to organize all aspects of the meeting. This will include the organization of a suitable venue, catering, refreshments and equipment to support the meeting. Anton also manages the budget, but it is close to the financial year-end and so he has a more restricted budget than he might like.

He **breaks down the job** into the following general tasks (note that, at this stage, they are listed in no particular order):

- select a venue which is geographically suitable for all those attending;
- check out participant location and preferences;
- liaise with the venue to arrange room layout, breakout rooms for smaller meetings and discussions;
- arrange a menu, based on participant needs;
- check out travel arrangements and organize these where necessary for some of the participants;
- send out details and instructions to participants;
- prepare the venue before the meeting.

Activity 39

10 mins

What does Anton need to do **before** deciding how to order the various tasks listed above?

_____

_____

_____

Anton needs to begin by reflecting on his experience in managing events, and **gathering all the relevant information** for the job. For example, it is likely that he will have built up a bank of information on suitable venues and caterers from previous events. This information might give an illustration of costs. He will also have to consider what other events he might have to organize before the end of the financial year, because of course this will have an effect on the budget. He may also wish to discuss the situation with his own staff, particularly if they are to be involved to any degree in this job. Anton will also need the list of participants, along with any special needs they might have.

For each of the tasks that Anton has listed, he will also need to consider the resources required and whether these resources are available. For example, he will know what his budget is, so this will influence his selection of venue, caterers and menu.

Having considered all the relevant information, Anton then gives each task an **identifier**, so he might label venue selection as Task A, while checking out participant location might be Task B, for example.

Once this has been done, he has to **order the tasks**. This is known as determining **precedence**, that is, decide which task needs to come before which. Can any tasks happen in parallel? A task that needs to be completed before another can begin is called the **predecessor**, and a task that can begin only once another one is completed is called the **successor**.

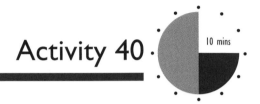

Activity 40

10 mins

Consider Anton's list of tasks in the example above. Give each of these tasks an identifier (A, B, C, and so on) and, using the chart below, see if you can work out which tasks need to take precedence over others. (They won't necessarily be done in alphabetical order. You might decide that Task C needs to be completed before Task B, for example.)

Task	Description	Predecessors

The answer to this Activity can be found on page 101.

Once this relationship between tasks has been worked out, Anton needs to **allocate necessary resources**. This should cover people, time, physical resources and, if relevant, money.

It is possible to extend the chart that you worked on in the above Activity to incorporate resource headings, identifying specified resources against each. For example, returning to the example of Anton:

Task	Description	People	Equipment	No. of days	Predecessors
A	Select venue	Anton and Jane	Telephone and word processor	0.5	B

From here you can begin to build your Gantt chart, or visual plan. The Gantt chart will immediately show you the amount of time needed to complete the whole project, as well as showing the time taken for each task. The visual plan will also indicate those tasks that can be done at the same time.

The figure below shows the outline of a Gantt chart.

Each task is represented as a bar, with each bar showing how long it will take to complete the task. Each bar is shown in relation to its defined predecessor and successor. See the illustration below.

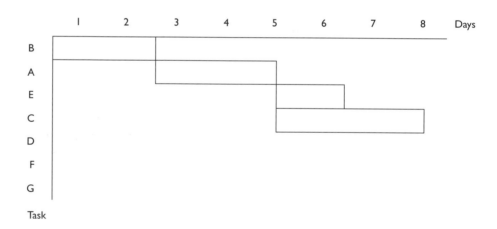

Activity 41 · 3 mins

Do you think Gantt charts might be useful in your job? Say briefly why you think so. Give examples of their use if appropriate.

_____

_____

You may feel that Gantt charts are not really applicable to your job, because you are not involved in complex planning decisions at this stage. However, it's useful to be aware of what they can do, particularly if your own line manager uses them in planning your work.

Self-assessment 3 · 10 mins

1 Give **two** reasons why diaries are useful.

_____

_____

_____

2 What are the three steps involved in planning a task using the list system?

- Step 1 Write down _____ _____

- Step 2 Decide _____

- Step 3 Decide _____

3 The four stages of preparing a Gantt chart are:

_____ into smaller tasks;

gather _____ in relation to the job, including people required and resource availability – including time;

place _____ – that is, decide what needs to be completed before another task can begin;

allocate the necessary _____ to each task.

Answers to these questions can be found on page 99.

6 Summary

■ **Plans cannot always be achieved**

But even plans that go wrong may be useful, and any plan helps to make better decisions when the unexpected occurs.

■ **Time logs**

- provide evidence on how you and your team are actually using time;
- contain information that may help you to get the idea of time management accepted in your workplace.

■ A **diary** helps with:

- longer-term planning;
- appointments;
- future commitments.

■ A **team diary** gives everyone in the team equal access to information that is relevant and important to all team members.

■ A **list** helps with:

- short-term planning;
- deciding the order of work;
- deciding how much time to spend on a job;
- keeping track of several jobs at once;
- planning the next step in a long series;
- jogging your memory.

■ A **Gantt chart** can help to:

- plan and manage complex tasks;
- make clear how timescales operate and what this means for those allocated to the various tasks.

Session D
The limitations of time management

▪ 1 Introduction

So far in this workbook we have stressed the importance of being able to manage your time, and that of your team members, more effectively. Of course, you may feel that much of what's been said is fine in principle, but be perhaps a bit sceptical as to whether it makes much difference in practice.

In this session, we look first at how you might carry out a time management exercise in practice in your area of work, first for yourself, and then for members of your team.

However, as we're all too well aware, plans in the abstract don't always work out in the real world, and it's important to be flexible in your thinking in the event that something unforeseen crops up – as it certainly will sooner or later. The session continues by looking at the different sorts of unforeseen contingencies that can arise, and how you might best approach these.

We then return to an issue raised earlier in this workbook – that of conflicting priorities and how these might be handled. Finally, we look at reviewing how we use our time.

▪ 2 Scheduling your own tasks

First of all use the management grid discussed in Session C to improve the organization of your own work.

Activity 42 ·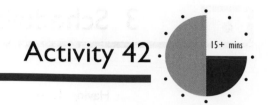

Using a separate sheet of paper, make yourself out a blank task list, using the headings below. (Alternatively, you can use cards, or a computer software package.)

No.	Task	Comment	Estimate

1   First list all the jobs you would like to get done tomorrow (or your next working day), in the second column in this list, just as we did for Tracy on page 60. Number the jobs in the first column, but don't fill in the time estimates yet.

2   Next, note down in the comments column the jobs in this list with a deadline or fixed time.

3   Now, plot the rest of the jobs on the management grid:

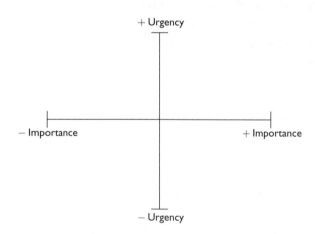

4   The next thing to do is to estimate the time needed for each task. Write in your estimates in the last column on your sheet.

5   Now you should be able to plan your schedule on a day plan. Use a new sheet, writing out the headings shown below. (If you have used cards, it is simply a matter of sorting the cards in the appropriate order.)

No.	Brief summary or name of task	Planned time

3 Scheduling team time

Having developed a more systematic schedule for your own time, we'll now move on to seeing how time management tools can be used for the benefit of your team.

Activity 43 · 60+ mins

Arrange a meeting of your team. Discuss and produce a list of tasks that need to be undertaken on a particular day, e.g. one day next week, or during a particular shift or time period. At the conclusion of the meeting each team member should have a detailed, individualized plan that shows:

■ the task itself, with brief description;
■ an identifier for each task;
■ estimated time to complete;
■ schedule of activity (refer to Tracy's plan on p. 64);
■ the level of importance/urgency attached to each task.

By adopting a group approach to this Activity, you will be producing schedules that are most relevant to all team members. At the same time, all the team members will be contributing their expertise in terms of the time that is actually needed to complete the tasks concerned.

One of the difficulties likely to be raised is the fact that scheduling in this way takes time. Scheduling itself becomes a time-consuming task. However, if we are able to combine our knowledge through such an approach, individuals can become more effective in estimating the time that is actually needed. Another important aspect of this type of exercise is that you are able to explore and agree what is really important and what is really urgent. If everyone on the team has an understanding of this, there is less likelihood of a clash between team members.

A shared understanding of the importance and urgency associated with the different tasks that a team has to achieve, will reduce the likelihood of conflicts between team members.

■ 4 The best-laid plans ...

Having completed your plans, you can set about getting through the items on your list. On some days you may be very successful: everything runs smoothly and every item on the list gets completed on time. Wonderful.

If you are like the rest of us, however, there will be days when your plans work out less well – or not at all.

Activity 44

Think back to a day when all your plans went wrong. What happened? Give a brief summary of events in the space below.

_____

_____

_____

_____

_____

_____

_____

_____

_____

_____

What usually happens is that something unexpected takes place. Here are five typical examples:

- There is an accident, and one of your team needs medical attention.
- A power failure stops your team working and means that the whole schedule of work has to be rearranged.
- Your plans assume that everyone will be at work; then two members of the team go sick.

- You seriously underestimate how long it will take to complete a certain job.
- Your manager has made plans which clash with yours.

We all know from experience that

plans often go wrong.

This doesn't mean that it isn't worth making plans. On the contrary,

when faced with the unexpected, a plan can help us make better decisions.

The reason for this is simple: even when events don't go according to schedule, then we can still consult the plan at any time, to help decide about the relative importance and urgency of the tasks ahead. That makes it much easier to modify the plan and to keep our priorities in mind.

5 Coping with the unexpected

'Death and taxes and childbirth! There's never any convenient time for any of them'. – Margaret Mitchell, *Gone with the Wind.*

If there's one thing certain, it is that the unexpected will occur.

When it does, a key question is whether the particular unplanned event is occurring too frequently. In other words,

is this a regular time-waster?

We will bear that question in mind as we examine the most common kinds of events that result in disrupted plans, and ask it again in the next section on reviewing the use of time.

5.1 Accidents

There are several things you can do about accidents and accident prevention.

Under your organization's health and safety policy you and your team should always be working to

If you would like more detailed information on this subject, see *Managing Health and Safety at Work* in this series.

reduce the likelihood of accidents taking place.

Even if accidents are very rare occurrences, you and your team should

know what to do if an accident happens.

In general, there are four things which must be done when any serious accident occurs:

■ The area must be made safe, so that no one else is in danger. If this isn't possible, everyone must be cleared from the area.

■ First aid must be given to anyone injured. If necessary, medical assistance must be summoned.

■ Any appropriate authority must be called: colleagues, the ambulance service, the fire brigade, the police – whichever is appropriate.

■ After the accident, an accident report must be filled out.

If an accident does occur, you will also need to

try to minimize any disruptions to your plans.

5.2 Machinery breakdown

Most people at work nowadays are dependent on machinery. If you are, it may be worth asking yourself whether the machinery you use is reliable enough.

To reduce the disruption caused by equipment failure, might you:

■ Press for more regular servicing of machines?
■ Make a case for replacing the machines?
■ Improve the call-out procedure, so that repair technicians arrive as quickly as possible?
■ Improve your workteam's knowledge so that everyone knows what to do if a breakdown occurs?

5.3 Absences

Problems may be caused by the absence of one of your team or the absence of someone else upon whom you rely.

Activity 45

3 mins

What do **you** do to minimize disruption caused by absences? What might you do? Give this a little thought and then make a note of at least **two** ideas.

_____

_____

_____

_____

_____

_____

_____

_____

_____

_____

Here are some suggestions – although not all of them may apply in your case:

- Foreseeable absences – doctors' or dentists' appointments for example – should of course be taken into account when planning work.
- An overlap of skills, so that one workteam member's work can be covered by another, may help to reduce the disruption caused by absences. Job rotation may increase the interest of workers, if it's possible to arrange.
- If you are forced to make last-minute changes to plans because of absences, you will obviously want to try to reschedule things so that the most important and urgent jobs still get done.
- If you are going to miss deadlines, it is usually better to notify people of this in advance.

5.4 Underestimating job times

Activity 46

3 mins

What can you do if you find that your work plans are regularly disrupted because of getting your estimates wrong?

_____

_____

_____

_____

If your estimates are regularly wrong, you can

■ leave some flexibility in your time plan, to allow for errors in estimates;
■ improve your skill at estimating by making a habit of comparing your estimates with the actual times taken. The time logs we discussed earlier would be useful here.

5.5 When new jobs arise

■ Before

Jean was in charge of a small team of clerical staff. Her manager was forever passing work to her marked 'urgent', and setting deadlines, which meant a great deal of disruption to the team's activities. Jean was a conscientious person who tried to get through all the work she was given. She sometimes grumbled and sometimes protested about the arrival of another 'urgent' piece of work, but she did her best to deal with it.

■ After

Jean started to keep a simple log of every item of work. She kept these on cards on her desk. If something urgent arrived when Jean and her team were very busy, she would take the current cards to show her manager. She would point out her workload and explain the effects on other work if the new task were undertaken.

Activity 47

3 mins

What effects do you think Jean's approach would have on her manager, and on the number of new items of work arriving on Jean's desk?

_____

_____

_____

_____

_____

This is a real-life example and the effects it had were that:

- fewer pieces of urgent work arrived, as the manager came to appreciate how much work Jean and her team were doing;
- the manager tended to consult Jean more about her workload, and to warn her when urgent and important projects were likely to arrive;
- Jean got more control over her own time and the time of her workteam.

This was because Jean had the facts at her fingertips and could argue on the basis of evidence and effects.

You may have suggested that the manager began to look more closely at how Jean organized her workteam. This might have happened, but Jean was confident that they were well organized. If the manager had shown an interest in this, Jean was prepared to state a case for more people and better equipment.

Another suggestion may have been that relations between Jean and her manager got worse. This might have happened if Jean had been aggressive or had refused to do urgent work, but she made her case very reasonably on the basis of the workload.

You may have suggested that it had no effect on the number of pieces of urgent work arriving. In fact, this tactic always has an effect **either** on the amount of urgent work arriving or on the resources which are made available to do it **and/or** the amount of notice given.

We have been looking at time planning and how you might make your plans more effective.

If much of your job is routine, then you will need to invest less time in planning, and the plans you make are more likely to be achievable.

For non-routine jobs, it is both:

■ more necessary to plan your time;
■ more difficult to do so accurately.

Do not be discouraged if at first you do not succeed. Begin with flexible plans and gradually aim to make them more accurate. Consider your plans very carefully and monitor and review them regularly.

In Jean's case above, she made her manager more aware of her time management problems, and that she needed to take more account of them, by keeping a simple log. Sometimes people can be more difficult to deal with, however.

5.6 Negotiating for better time management

As we discussed in the previous session, you can't ignore other people when deciding how to get more control of your time. Sometimes, other people can get in the way of your plans. Other people may be one of the main limitations to the effective use of time management techniques. Consider this case.

> Andreas was a team leader in the design studio of a publishing company, where his team members were specialists in typography, illustration, page layout, and so on. He had been in this job for two months when he became interested in time management as a solution to his problems. He kept time logs, drew up schedules and tried a series of new systems to try to get control of his time and that of his team, but enjoyed only limited success.
>
> It turned out that the studio manager encouraged people to approach Andreas's team members directly to get jobs done, especially when projects were late or small amendments were required. The manager often did this himself. This meant that Andreas often did not know what his team were doing and his own work plans were often disrupted.
>
> The studio manager would not listen to Andreas's reasonable arguments about the importance of particular jobs and wouldn't support any new system Andreas proposed.

The causes of the problem here were to do with:

- **Structure:** Who had the power to give instructions to Andreas's team? Andreas thought all requests for work should go through him, but the previous supervisor on the job had obviously allowed anyone to give his team instructions.

- **Personalities:** The studio manager would not listen to Andreas's reasoned arguments.

Activity 48

3 mins

What do you think Andreas could do about this?

_____

_____

_____

_____

_____

There are a number of options for Andreas, some of them quite drastic.

He could look for another job, or have a showdown with the studio manager. Andreas, however, thought these measures were too extreme.

Andreas decided that he could:

- work on building a good relationship with his workteam, so that they would keep him informed of what was happening;
- talk to his team about priorities and get agreement about the importance and urgency of matters;
- talk to the people who make demands on his team to ensure that the demands go through him, so that he can try to foresee some of the demands;
- work on developing a good relationship with the studio manager and to encourage him to consult Andreas more;
- deal with the stress, which is the main result of his time management problems.

These are all practical options. Check to see if your suggestions were similar to these. Can you see why it is reasonable to try to put all of them into effect?

Andreas's problems were **regular** disruptions. It was necessary, therefore, to invest some time in trying to reduce the likelihood of them occurring and to **reduce** the impact of the disruptions when they did occur.

Andreas had to accept that:

- getting control of his time was going to be a slow and gradual process;
- most of the work was going to involve talking with and persuading other people.

So, resolving time management problems can often involve **negotiation** or **conflict** even when we have sorted out our own priorities.

6 Reviewing the use of time

In the previous section we looked at the sorts of things that can and do go wrong in the course of a working day, and discussed some of the ways that you can deal with disruptions when they do occur. In this section we encourage you to reflect on why they happen, and how you might take steps to reduce their impact in the future.

When reviewing how we use time it is important to consider:

- the SMARTness of the original objectives;
- scheduling;
- disruptions.

6.1 Revisiting objectives

Objectives will be time bound, and as indicated earlier it is essential that there be review points built into objectives to ensure that any necessary changes can take place at an appropriate time. Where there is a formal appraisal or performance review process you and the team member concerned will consider the original objectives and explore how far these have been achieved.

By considering the SMARTness of the objective you and your team member, or indeed you and your own manager, can decide where any problems might lie. How clear was the original objective? Have the necessary resources been available? Was the objective relevant? Or has the relevance changed, where the organization has changed its priorities or needs?

In revisiting objectives it is essential that there be a way of actually amending these. There is no point in keeping the same objectives where all manner of issues have arisen, rendering them unachievable or irrelevant.

6.2 Reviewing schedules

One of the most common problems with scheduling is that we underestimate the actual time that it will take to complete a job. In the previous section we looked at **what** you could do if you get your estimates wrong. Here, we ask **why** this happens in the first place.

Activity 49

Give two reasons **why** we might underestimate job times.

_____

_____

Reasons for underestimating job times might include:

■ The desire to support colleagues further along in the work process. We all worry that if we take too long in our work we will stop others doing what they need to do.
■ We base our estimates on a few occasions where there were no interruptions or disruptions to the job. We might remember where things have gone really well and decide to use these times as our benchmarks.
■ A fear of seeming less than proficient in any aspect of our job. We might worry that others believe we do not have the necessary capability to do the job.
■ Pressure of tighter deadlines, where this pressure is imposed by the organization.

When we review work schedules we need to be honest in stating where we have underestimated time. If you are aware that team members are underestimating the time needed then you may want to determine the reasons. If the team member is worried, perhaps for one of the reasons stated above, you will need to show your support. Stress the importance of estimating correctly, showing what can go wrong if time is underestimated.

Another factor that must be considered when reviewing schedules is where time was saved. Where a particular process is regularly shown to take less time than was originally estimated then this time could be allotted elsewhere – for example, to tasks where time has been regularly underestimated.

6.3 Reviewing disruptions

Look back over section 5 again. What are the disruptions that you have experienced on a regular basis? Are they disruptions that could not have been foreseen? Are they disruptions that happen all too regularly and have become likely? Do you and your team regularly spend time on the same types of disruption?

If you answer yes to any of these questions then it may be the case that what was once an occasional disruption has now become a regular time-waster, or time thief. Where this type of disruption cannot be dealt with through a change of process or the implementation of a policy or procedure (for example the introduction of a regular maintenance schedule to a problematic piece of equipment) then you and your team will need to consider how to tackle this issue through planning.

Activity 50

Reflect on your own schedule for the past week. What were the disruptions that affected your schedule on more than two occasions? List these below.

What steps, if any, can you take in the future to reduce this type of disruption?

_____

_____

_____

Obviously the steps that you considered will depend upon the nature of the disruption. However, it is important that we do not just assume that disruptions must happen – they will. It is important that we consider the nature of the disruption and the reality of its impact, and find practical methods for managing this.

A thorough review of the original objectives, our schedules and the nature of any disruptions to our schedules will help us to take action and so maximize the time available to ourselves and our team.

So, the scope of time management is very broad. It embraces:

- making decisions about your goals and objectives;
- analysing demands on your time;

- analysing how your time is spent;
- planning your time;
- negotiating with others over how you spend your time;
- reviewing the use of your time.

Self-assessment 4 · ⏱ 10 mins

1   Pauline, Sahail and Rick are suspicious of your plans for time management, and each has an objection. Briefly explain how you would counter each one.

   a Pauline: 'Machinery breakdown is just one of those things: you can't plan for it'.

   _____

   _____

   b Sahail: 'Absences aren't foreseeable – there's nothing you can do about them'.

   _____

   _____

   c Rick: 'Plans are useful – until they go wrong'.

   _____

   _____

2   Select the **two** correct statements from the list below, and explain why the other two are wrong.

   Time management embraces:
   a analysing how your time is spent;
   b learning what to do in the event of an accident;
   c planning your time effectively;
   d confusing your manager with time logs and management grids.

   Answers to these questions can be found on page 99.

7 Summary

- Scheduling your time and that of your team members is important because:

  - it helps you achieve your objectives actively, rather than responding to the demands of others;
  - it gives you a yardstick against which to measure actual performance;
  - you can use the practical knowledge of your team to make realistic estimates of how long things actually take;
  - it can help to sort out priorities and reduce conflicts between team members or between you and other managers.

- If something can go wrong, it will. Plans help us to cope better with the unexpected.

- Deal with disruptions of plans by:

  - having systems in place for dealing with accidents, breakdowns and absences;
  - finding a longer-term solution which reduces the likelihood of their happening;
  - reducing the possibility of damage when they do occur;
  - negotiating with others.

Performance checks

▣ 1 Quick quiz

Jot down the answers to the following questions on *Achieving Objectives Through Time Management*.

Question 1   Write down a brief definition of 'managing time'. One or two sentences will do.

_____

_____

Question 2   List two kinds of 'activity trap'.

_____

_____

Question 3   What's the difference between a crisis and a high priority task?

_____

_____

Question 4   'If you have a time management problem, you will certainly know you have.' Is this statement true, or false?

_____

_____

Question 5   Write down two undesirable results of crisis management.

_____

_____

Question 6   We discussed three steps for getting out of an activity trap. Two were: 'Set goals' and 'Choose priorities'. What was the third?

_____

_____

Question 7   In the stages of decision making: knowledge, objectives, alternatives, look ahead, action, what does the first stage – knowledge – mean?

_____

_____

Question 8   What does 'look ahead' mean?

_____

_____

Question 9   What are SMART objectives?

_____

_____

Question 10   Give an example of a habit that can help in the management of time.

_____

_____

Question 11   Define 'urgent'.

_____

_____

Question 12   Define 'important'.

_____

_____

Question 13   On the time management grid, what are the risks associated with tasks that appear in the 'high urgency and high importance' quadrant?

_____

_____

Question 14   On the time management grid, what are the risks associated with tasks that appear in the 'low urgency and low importance' quadrant?

_____

_____

Question 15   Name two kinds of people who might benefit from a list system.

_____

_____

Question 16   Lastly, how can plans help us to deal with unplanned events?

_____

_____

Answers to these questions can be found on page 101.

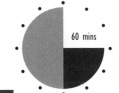

60 mins

☐• 2 Workbook assessment

Read the following case incident, and then deal with the questions that follow. Write your answers on a separate sheet of paper.

Petra was a slave to the telephone. Whoever called, Petra would put herself out to deal with the query or problem herself, and straight away. She was good at this job and many of the customers would ask for her specifically, when they wanted someone to take action. Trouble was, Petra was a girl who couldn't say no to people who wanted her help. After a while, she was getting more calls than all of the rest of the people in the office combined. People would come to her not only with genuine queries, but just to burden her with their problems. Petra would try to deal with problems that had not the remotest connection with her department or her job.

She liked being the centre of attention and being indispensable, but her phone line was blocked for most of the day and customers with real problems, relevant to Petra's section, couldn't get through.

Answer the following questions about Petra's case. You do not need to write more than three or four sentences in reply to each question.

1   Would you say that Petra has a time management problem? Give a reason for your answer.

2   To which of our descriptions of activity traps does Petra's situation most closely correspond?

3   What do you think are the possible outcomes if Petra continues in this vein? Is it good or bad for Petra? Is it good or bad for the organization?

For Questions 4, 5 and 6, imagine that you are Petra's team leader.

4   What possible courses of action do you think you have, based on what you know about the case? List three possible options.

5   Now consider each of your options, and decide what you think the consequences might be.

6   Based on your analysis, and assuming your objectives include making your team more efficient and making the best use of Petra's talents, make a decision on what action to take. Explain briefly why you have made that decision.

Reflect and review

1 Reflect and review

Now that you have completed your work on *Achieving Objectives Through Time Management*, let us review our workbook objectives.

■ At the end of this workbook you should be better able to identify ways of increasing efficiency and effectiveness through better time management.

We all have the same amount of time in a day, but some people seem to make better use of their time than others. If you can identify your own patterns of working, you should be able to modify them, so that your efficiency and effectiveness improves. We talked about certain kinds of 'activity trap': crisis management, 'responding to demands', and the treadmill. Are your hopes and ambitions ensnared in one of these, preventing you from gaining control of your working life? Take some bold decisions. Get out of the trap, and organize your time so that you can achieve more, and reach higher standards.

Answer the following questions:

■ If you feel you act as a crisis manager too frequently, what plans do you have to discuss this state of affairs with your workteam and/or your manager?

_____

_____

■ If you spend all your time 'responding to demands', how do you intend to start controlling your own time more by deciding your own priorities?

_____

_____

■ If you believe you are on a treadmill for part or all of your working life, how do you intend changing your approach, your priorities and your outlook?

_____

_____

_____

■ At the end of this workbook you should be better able to differentiate between the demands on the time available, and to agree and set priorities.

Perhaps you agree that slotting tasks into the quadrants of the management grid is a useful way of categorizing them. The distinction between 'important' and 'urgent' is fairly fundamental, but frequently overlooked. So many people get their priorities confused, because they tend to respond to urgent demands on their time, and to set aside important jobs until they find themselves facing a crisis. If there's one thing that you can usefully do after reading this workbook, it is to get in the habit of differentiating between tasks, and assigning them a label: 'a waste of time', 'genuine crisis', 'quick and simple', or 'planning task'.

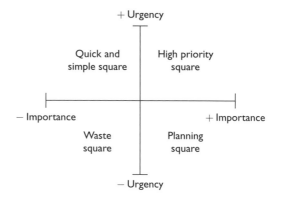

■ In which quadrant do you spend most of your time?

_____

_____

_____

■ Where would you like to be spending more of your time? [Hint: try to head south-east.]

_____

_____

_____

The next workbook objective is to:

■ Realize more of you and your team's goals by utilizing available time more effectively.

Knowing what you and your team need to achieve will help to concentrate the mind. People who have a clear idea of their goals are more likely to achieve them. Determining which part of your work, and of course your team's work, is important in reaching those goals, and focusing on those tasks will support you and the team in accomplishing most things that you set your minds to.

■ Write down two goals that you believe are important both to you and all members of your team

_____

_____

_____

_____

■ What must you all do to reach these goals?

_____

_____

_____

_____

The last workbook objective is to:

■ Employ appropriate time management techniques that can support the use of your own and your team's time.

We are all aware of different techniques for managing time. Where you and your team adopt methods that are appropriate to your needs, you are more likely to make more effective use of the time available. A shared and agreed approach to planning, scheduling and reviewing the use of time will enable positive and productive action to be taken, using that all too limited resource – time.

■ How can you make sure that your own and your team's objectives are SMART?

_____

_____

_____

_____

■ When will you take action to improve your own and your team's approach to managing time?

_____

_____

2 Action Plan

Use this plan to develop further for yourself a course of action you want to take. Make a note in the left-hand column of the issues or problems you want to tackle, and then decide what you intend to do, and make a note in column 2.

The resources you need might include time, materials, information or money. You may need to negotiate for some of them, but they could be something easily acquired, like half an hour of somebody's time, or a chapter of a book. Put whatever you need in column 3. No plan means anything without a timescale, so put a realistic target completion date in column 4.

Finally, describe the outcome you want to achieve as a result of this plan, whether it is for your own benefit or advancement, or a more efficient way of doing things.

Desired outcomes				
1 Issues	2 Action	3 Resources	4 Target completion	
Actual outcomes				

3 Extensions

Extension 1

Book	*The Time Management Pocketbook*
Authors	Ian Fleming
Edition	4th edition 1997
Publisher	Management Pocketbooks
	ISBN 1870471539

Extension 2

Book	*Time Management for Unmanageable People*
Author	Ann McGee-Cooper, Duane Trammell
Edition	1994
Publisher	Bantam Books
	ISBN 0553370715

Extension 3

Book	*Perfect Time Management*
Author	Edward Johns
Edition	1999
Publisher	Arrow
	ISBN 0099410044

Extension 4

Book	*Effective Time Management – How to Save Time and Use it Wisely*
Author	John Adair
Edition	1988
Publisher	Pan
	ISBN: 0330302299

Extension 5

Book	*Getting Things Done*
Author	David Allen
Edition	2002
Publisher	Piatkus Books
	ISBN 0749922648

All these books are interesting and easy to read. You should only need to get hold of one of them.

These extensions can be taken up via your ILM Centre. They will either have them or will arrange that you have access to them. However, it may be more convenient to check out the materials with your personnel or training people at work – they may well give you access. There are other good reasons for approaching your own people; for example, they will become aware of your interest and you can involve them in your development.

4 Answers to self-assessment questions

1 a Managing time means getting more CONTROL over how we spend our time and making sensible DECISIONS about how we use it.
   b To become a crisis manager, simply do NOTHING. A crisis will occur sooner or later.
   c Managing time means making the BEST USE of your time.
   d The way out of an activity trap is to set PRIORITIES: choose GOALS; make DECISIONS.

2 The two incorrect statements are:

   c In order to manage time better, we need to think about what others would like us to achieve, and who stands in the way of us achieving it.
   Reason: In order to manage time better, we need to think about what **we** would like to achieve, and **what** stands in the way of us achieving it.
   d It is natural to try to avoid a crisis because nobody enjoys them.
   Reason: Many people enjoy crises; it is often more 'natural' to regard the crisis as inevitable.

3 The two most correct statements are that activity traps:

   b include firefighting, the treadmill and 'responding to demands';
   c can cause stress, frustration, errors and missed opportunities;

   The incorrect statements are that activity traps:

   a are routine ways of working from which there's no escape.
   Reason: This is incorrect because there is a way of escape.
   d help us to recognize our goals.
   Reason: This is incorrect because the opposite is true; activity traps stop us recognizing our goals.

4 Managers and TEAM leaders are in danger of falling into activity TRAPS, one of which is the TREADMILL, in which the person concerned faces an endless succession of routine TASKS. To TAKE control of your TIME, you need to use TECHNIQUES designed to help you get out of these TRAPS. In the case of the TREADMILL, TRAINING may be the answer, as it could give you the skills to tackle more interesting TASKS.

Reflect and review

Self-assessment 2 on page 50

1 The stages of decision making can be written as:

KNOWLEDGE
OBJECTIVES
ALTERNATIVES
LOOKING AHEAD
ACTION

2 a Using time badly may be caused by bad HABITS; good habits can help people USE TIME WELL.

b There is a DANGER that tasks that are URGENT BUT NOT IMPORTANT may take up too much time.

c If its EFFECTS OR RESULTS change, a task may CHANGE in importance.

d Only you can DECIDE how to RESPOND TO DEMANDS on your time.

e You won't ACHIEVE YOUR OBJECTIVES if you simply respond to the demands of others.

f If a task is NOT URGENT, it may never get done at all.

g Question: should you use your TIME on tasks that have NO URGENCY OR IMPORTANCE?

h The correct TIMING OF A DECISION depends on getting the best INFORMATION you can.

i The danger is that tasks that are BOTH URGENT AND IMPORTANT may not get done very well.

j The PASSING OF TIME has no effect on the importance of something.

3

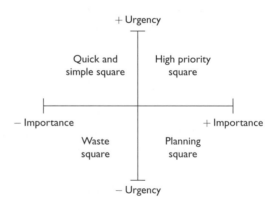

4 a A job which is nearing its deadline: B.

b A job which has suddenly become more important, because of a management decision: A.

c A job which was never very important, but now is hardly worth doing at all, because of a change of priorities: D.

d A job which has increased dramatically in both urgency and importance: C.

Self-assessment 3 on page 69

1   Diaries can help you and your team to:

- Plan your own and your team's time;
- keep your promises;
- keep appointments.

2   The three steps in planning a task using the list system are:

- Step 1 Write down a list of all the things you want to do (that day, say).
- Step 2 Decide in what order you will tackle the items on the list.
- Step 3 Decide how long you will spend on each item.

3   The four stages of preparing a Gantt chart are to:

- **break the job down** into smaller tasks;
- gather **all the information necessary** in relation to the job, including people required and resource availability – including time;
- place **the tasks in order** – that is, decide what needs to be completed before another task can begin;
- allocate the necessary **resources** to each task.

Self-assessment 4 on page 85

1   a There are a number of things you can plan for in connection with machinery breakdown, including: getting the machines regularly serviced; putting an efficient system in place so that repairs will be made quickly; improving the knowledge of the people using the machines, so they will know what to do should a breakdown occur; replacing worn-out machines.

   b Some absences are foreseeable – such as dentists' appointments – and should be notified beforehand. In addition, you can make plans for absences by:

- ensuring you have an overlap of skills, so that one workteam member's work can be covered by another, which may help to reduce the disruption caused by absences;
- organizing a system for getting a temporary replacement if absenteeism is a regular problem.

   c Plans nearly always go wrong, but unless you make plans you have no hope of controlling events. The trick is to be flexible, and modify your plans as circumstances change.

2   Time management embraces:
   a analysing how your time is spent;
   c planning your time effectively;

   It **does not** embrace:

   b learning what to do in the event of an accident – even though this is useful.
   d confusing your manager with time logs and management grids – the idea is not to confuse, but to produce constructive evidence of how you spend your time.

● 5 Answers to activities

**Activity 15
on page 23**

The kinds of demands placed on the managers in the other two cases can be described like this:

- Responding to demands
  - A large number of demands, of different kinds.
  - Many of the demands are about small matters.
  - The demands come from management, the workteam and other people.
  - Longer-term planning may be ignored.

- The treadmill
  - A large volume of demands, none of them very interesting.
  - The demands are mostly of the same type – there is a high workload, without the variety of the crisis manager or responding to demands.
  - The demands seem to be regular and predictable.
  - Longer-term goals may be neglected.

You may have made other points about the demands made upon these people, but we hope you'll agree that ours are also true.

**Activity 25
on page 41**

The job can be plotted moving up the grid, as shown:

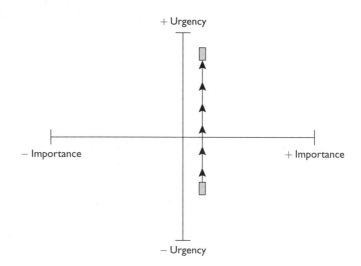

**Activity 40
on page 67**

If, as we did, you simply identified the tasks in alphabetically in the same order as they were listed in the example, the outcome may have looked like this:

Task	Description	Predecessor(s)
B	Check out participant location and preferences	
A	Select a venue	B
E	Check out and make travel arrangements	A, B
C	Liaise with venue	A, B
D	Arrange a menu	A, B
F	Send out details	A, B, D and E
G	Prepare venue	A–F

Clearly, a number of smaller tasks are implied within each of the above, but certainly it will be impossible to send out details (F) if the venue has not been selected, travel arrangements made and the menu finalized.

6 Answers to the quick quiz

Answer 1 Your definition should have included the words 'control' and 'decisions' – something like: 'Managing time means controlling how you spend your time and making decisions about it.'

Answer 2 You might have mentioned 'crisis management' (or fire-fighting), 'responding to demands' and 'the treadmill'.

Answer 3 We defined a high priority as something that is: very urgent and must be dealt with immediately; very important and should be given a great deal of attention, or thought; is both urgent and important: it must be done immediately and done well; takes precedence over everything else. A crisis was defined as 'a crucial state of affairs, requiring urgent action, whose outcome will have a decisive effect for better or worse'. Many people use these terms to mean the same thing, but if there is a difference, it is that a crisis is rather more serious and important.

Answer 4   It is false. You may or may not realize you have a time management problem. Usually you won't.

Answer 5   You may have mentioned: stress, mistakes, fatigue and high cost.

Answer 6   The third was 'Make decisions'.

Answer 7   'Knowledge' means gathering all the facts you can and checking they are correct, before you start.

Answer 8   'Look ahead' means to think out the results of the alternative proposals you have put up, before you take action.

Answer 9   Objectives that are SMART are **S**pecific, **M**easurable, **A**chievable, **R**elevant and **T**ime bound.

Answer 10   The example we gave in the workbook was that of someone who deliberately got into the habit of setting aside some time each day for longer-term planning. You may have a different example.

Answer 11   Something is urgent when it demands our immediate attention.

Answer 12   Something is important when it has considerable significance or consequence.

Answer 13   We are in danger of not doing the job well.

Answer 14   We are in danger of doing the job – which probably isn't worth doing at all.

Answer 15   Managers in charge of a general duties team; managers who have to relate to a large number of people; managers who are involved in long-range projects; managers who have poor memories.

Answer 16   In making plans, we identify important jobs. When a plan is interrupted by an unplanned event, a decision has to be made: is the new event more important or urgent than the planned event? Without a plan in the first place, these decisions are therefore much harder to make.

7 Certificate

Completion of this certificate by an authorized person shows that you have worked through all the parts of this workbook and satisfactorily completed the assessments. The certificate provides a record of what you have done that may be used for exemptions or as evidence of prior learning against other nationally certificated qualifications.

superseries

Achieving Objectives
Through Time Management

....

has satisfactorily completed this workbook

Name of signatory   ....

Position   ....

Signature   ....

Date   ....

Official stamp

Pergamon
Flexible
Learning

Fifth Edition

superseries

FIFTH EDITION

Workbooks in the series:

Achieving Objectives Through Time Management	978-0-08-046415-2
Building the Team	978-0-08-046412-1
Coaching and Training your Work Team	978-0-08-046418-3
Communicating One-to-One at Work	978-0-08-046438-1
Developing Yourself and Others	978-0-08-046414-5
Effective Meetings for Managers	978-0-08-046439-8
Giving Briefings and Making Presentations in the Workplace	978-0-08-046436-7
Influencing Others at Work	978-0-08-046435-0
Introduction to Leadership	978-0-08-046411-4
Managing Conflict in the Workplace	978-0-08-046416-9
Managing Creativity and Innovation in the Workplace	978-0-08-046441-1
Managing Customer Service	978-0-08-046419-0
Managing Health and Safety at Work	978-0-08-046426-8
Managing Performance	978-0-08-046429-9
Managing Projects	978-0-08-046425-1
Managing Stress in the Workplace	978-0-08-046417-6
Managing the Effective Use of Equipment	978-0-08-046432-9
Managing the Efficient Use of Materials	978-0-08-046431-2
Managing the Employment Relationship	978-0-08-046443-5
Marketing for Managers	978-0-08-046974-4
Motivating to Perform in the Workplace	978-0-08-046413-8
Obtaining Information for Effective Management	978-0-08-046434-3
Organizing and Delegating	978-0-08-046422-0
Planning Change in the Workplace	978-0-08-046444-2
Planning to Work Efficiently	978-0-08-046421-3
Providing Quality to Customers	978-0-08-046420-6
Recruiting, Selecting and Inducting New Staff in the Workplace	978-0-08-046442-8
Solving Problems and Making Decisions	978-0-08-046423-7
Understanding Change in the Workplace	978-0-08-046424-4
Understanding Culture and Ethics in Organizations	978-0-08-046428-2
Understanding Organizations in their Context	978-0-08-046427-5
Understanding the Communication Process in the Workplace	978-0-08-046433-6
Understanding Workplace Information Systems	978-0-08-046440-4
Working with Costs and Budgets	978-0-08-046430-5
Writing for Business	978-0-08-046437-4

For prices and availability please telephone our order helpline +44 (0) 1865 474010
or email directorders@elsevier.com